INSIGHT COMPACT GUIDE

SINGAPORE

Compact Guide: Singapore is the ideal quick-reference guide to the Asian city-state. It tells you all you need to know about Singapore's attractions, from Raffles Hotel to Orchard Road, Chinatown to Little India, and Arab Street to Sentosa Island, taking in the city's parks, gardens and other recreation spots on the way, as well as providing detailed information on where to shop and dine.

This is one of 120 Compact Guides, which combine the interests and enthusiasms of two of the world's best known information providers: Insight Guides, whose titles have set the standard for visual travel guides since 1970, and Discovery Channel, the world's premier source of nonfiction television programming.

P9-CKF-911

Star Attractions

An instant reference to some of Singapore's most popular tourist attractions to help you on your way.

Raffles Hotel p26

Orchard Road p27–31

Chinatown p32–7

Thian Hock Keng Temple p34

Little India p38–41

Arab Street p42–3

Sentosa Island p44–7

Geylang Serai Market p51

Merlion p23

Mandai Orchid Gardens p57

Harbour boats p58–9

SINGAPORE

Singapore – Southeast Asia's City-state

Opposite: Stamford Raffles remembered

Singapore's name derives from an optical illusion. According to legend, at some time in the 14th century, when the island was part of the huge Sri Vijaya empire, a visiting prince from Sumatra thought he saw a lion in the middle of a tropical rainforest where the predator, normally at home on open plains, would never go. The prince was so certain he had seen a lion that he called the island at the southern tip of Malaysia 'Singa Pura' or 'Lion City'. The merlion, a mythical creature with a lion's head and a fish's tail, later became the state symbol of Singapore.

Merlion – symbol of Singapore

The island slumbered on until the 19th century when an Englishman named Stamford Raffles identified the settlement, with its naturally sheltered harbour, as being of great strategic maritime importance. On 6 February 1819 he purchased the land from the then ruler, the Sultan of Johor, and obtained permission to establish a trading post for the British East India Company. At last the English had gained a foothold in this part of the world which until then had been firmly under Dutch control. As a free port, Singapore attracted commercial vessels from all over the world. More and more Europeans, particularly the English, saw good trading prospects here and settled on the tropical island in large numbers. Cheap labour was urgently required and so hard-working Chinese and Indians, eager to escape the poverty and hunger of their homeland, were recruited.

5

By the middle of the 19th century, Europe and Asia had been brought closer together by the advent of steamships, the telegraph and also the opening of the Suez Canal. Even the doubters had to admit it: the British had got a bargain, quite apart from the strategic importance of gaining a military presence in the Far East. Because of its strong defensive installations, Singapore was regarded as virtually impregnable – until 1942, that is, when it took Japanese troops only a few weeks to capture the British base. Using the road and rail causeway from Malaysia to Singapore, the unstoppable enemy soldiers arrived on, of all things, bicycles.

Since then, something remarkable has happened in Singapore. No new arrival at the city's ultra-modern airport today can fail to be impressed: polished marble, fountains, orchids, soft upholstery, tidy rows of shops and spotlessly clean toilets. The slums, epidemics, poverty, crime and poor hygiene that some first-time visitors still expect to find in Southeast Asia have been eradicated. The food is safe to eat, even from the hawker stalls, and the streets are virtually crime-free. Visitors now marvel at the orderliness, the new residential districts, the skyscrapers and the restored streets.

Singapore today

Location and landscape

The island state of Singapore lies about 137km (85 miles) north of the equator, just off the southern tip of Malaysia. It is linked to the Johor by the 1.1-km (½-mile) Causeway at Woodlands and a 1.9-km (1-mile) second road link at Tuas. About 52 islands also belong to Singapore, the largest being Tekong, Ubin and Sentosa. The main island measures 23km (14 miles) from north to south and 42km (26 miles) from east to west. The landscape is gently undulating, with large parts no more than 15m (50ft) above sea level. Bukit Timah Hill at the centre of the island reaches 162.5m (534ft). Granite and other hard rocks determined the original landscape. Steep inclines of sedimentary rock dominate the west and southwest, e.g. Mount Faber. Apart from a few cliffs, the coastline is generally flat, although in some places its course has been changed considerably by man. Harbours have been created, mangrove swamps drained and the natural contours altered by bulldozers. There are a few small watercourses, but many canals drain off the heavy tropical rainfall. The longest river, the Sungei Seletar, is 15km (9 miles) long.

Climate and when to go

The tropical climate of Singapore is hot and humid with the average temperature hovering around 27°C (80°F). During the daytime, it often goes above 30°C (86°F), but there are no great fluctuations. Humidity is high, and varies between 64 and 96 percent. The northeast monsoon blows from December to March, and the southwest from June to September, but the wind speeds are light, all year round. Spectacular thunderstorms occur frequently between the monsoons, in April–May and October–November. Most offices, shopping centres, underground train stations and homes are air-conditioned and this makes it easier for Singaporeans to cope with the sweltering temperatures.

Flora and fauna

It is hard to believe, but the island of Singapore was once a tropical jungle. When Stamford Raffles and his crew dropped anchor off the coast in the early 19th century, they found impenetrable mangrove forests lining the shore. Natural vegetation now only occurs in conservation areas such as the Bukit Timah Nature Reserve. Hardwood trees up to 40m (130ft) tall remain in the surviving primeval forest, but the mangroves have largely disappeared.

Despite all the building and construction, Singapore is not about to become a concrete desert. In addition to its nature reserves, the city-state has numerous parks and gardens, and amid the sea of houses, Singapore's huge

Exploring Bukit Timah

Botanic Gardens has a large collection of plants and trees. Nevertheless, about 80 percent of the species growing here are not native. The lush bougainvillea which adorn the cityscape originated in South America, while the rubber tree comes from Brazil.

Botanic Gardens

Singapore is famous for its rare and colourful orchids, many of which are cultivated and then exported. Packaged flowers can be bought at the airport and taken home as presents or souvenirs. Flower lovers should visit the breathtakingly beautiful Mandai Orchid Gardens *(see page 57)*.

It is often difficult to identify certain orchids as there are so many different shapes and colours. Some have brightly coloured, fleshy petals, others flower modestly in the background. Many of them embed their roots very firmly in the bark of a tree. One typical feature of orchids is the 'labellum', the most striking and most unusual of the six petals. 'Vanda Miss Joaquim', the national orchid of Singapore, has a deep violet labellum. When a new hybrid is developed, the Singaporean botanists often have difficulty knowing what to call it and famous visitors to the city often discover that a new orchid has been christened after them.

One of many species at the Mandai Orchid Gardens

Most of the native fauna live in the natural woodland. Lemurs and squirrels are plentiful, as are lizards, snakes, frogs and bats, but Singapore is particularly proud of its birdlife. Over 320 different species have been recorded, most of them migratory birds from the northern hemisphere, which overwinter near the equator.

While lions have never lived on the island, tigers certainly have, but they were mercilessly hunted to extinction during the 19th century. The last freely roaming tiger was shot in the Raffles Hotel billiard room in 1902; it had escaped from a travelling circus. When Singapore zoo *(see page 57)* was opened in 1974, tigers were re-introduced, but they are locked away inside a secure enclosure.

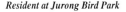

Resident at Jurong Bird Park

A new generation of Moslems

Population

Singapore has made remarkably rapid economic strides and has become a wealthy and independent state. The efficient infrastructure has proved extremely attractive to multinationals and the city is often held up as a model for other countries of Southeast Asia. In fact, some of the city-state's social policies are arousing much interest among European politicians. This considerable feat owes much to the country's political structure, which actually bears little resemblance to Western concepts of democracy and consensus. Before condemning the dominance of the ruling classes, however, outsiders should try to see Singapore in the context of the culture and attitudes of the various Asian races that live here.

'Many races, one nation, one Singapore' – this was the slogan used in the celebrations that marked the republic's 25th birthday in 1990 and it embodies the wish of the island's different races to work together for the prosperity of the nation – no easy task for 3.9 million people inhabiting a tiny island, particularly when the cultural heritage is so diverse. The overwhelming majority are Chinese (77 percent), the remainder are Malays (14 percent), Indians (8 percent) and other ethnic groups, such as Eurasians (1 percent).

Only the Malays can describe themselves as natives, as for hundreds of years their ancestors plied between the Malaysian mainland and the island. When in 1819 Stamford Raffles made his first trip up the Singapore River, all he discovered was a small Malay village with about 150 inhabitants, but that was soon to change. It was beside the mouth of the river that the first settlement was established. Immigrants flocked here in response to invitations from the prospering trading post and many came in the hope of finding work and a decent livelihood.

Malays were the first to arrive, followed by migrants from the Dutch-controlled Melaka region. Balinese, Javanese and Bugis (from the island of Celebes, now Sulawesi) also came in large numbers. Common cultural and religious strands between the islanders and the Malays quickly united these settlers.

The new arrivals from China, however, did not form such an homogeneous group. The first junk with Chinese immigrants arrived in February 1821. Most came from the southern provinces of mainland China, and they were known as Hokkiens, Teochews and Cantonese or Hakkas, depending on their native region and spoken dialect. The Hokkiens are still by far the largest dialect group. All of them wished to retain their cultural identity, whether by continuing their traditional professions and religious rituals or by preparing their food according to ancient customs. Initially, it was only the menfolk who ventured to the island and, of course, many of them then married Malay women.

The children from these relationships were called *Peranakans* or Straits Chinese, since their mothers originated from the Straits Settlements, as Melaka, Penang and Singapore were known. They were the first Asians to speak English and to adopt Western customs. Their staunch loyalty to the colony led some to describe them cynically as the 'King's Chinese'. Inevitably, the *nonyas* (women) and *babas* (men) created a double culture. 'Inside Chinese, outside Malay' is one description that has been applied to the Peranakans, although they no longer exist as a distinct sector of the population. The often wealthy Peranakan families in Singapore, e.g. on Emerald Hill *(see Route 2, page 29)*, often left behind homes whose distinctive architectural style and coloured tiles on the facade were typically Chinese.

The Chinese make up the majority

Around the middle of the 19th century, many Chinese women emigrated to Singapore with the encouragement of the British colonial authorities. By 1867 some 67 percent of the island's inhabitants were Chinese. In order to keep arguments and interracial conflict to a minimum, from the very beginning Raffles segregated the various ethnic groups. In Chinatown, the different dialect groups were allocated certain streets. Although the Chinese can speak Cantonese, Teochew etc, the Singapore authorities regard Mandarin as the official language of the Chinese community. English is the language of business and administration, but Malay and Tamil are also classified as official languages.

Little India *(see pages 38–41)* is the name given to the quarter initially settled by Indians. The first Indian settlers were immigrants either from the southern part of India or Sri Lanka. Several hundred of them were transported

Residents of Little India

here by the British in 1823 and were housed in camps while working on roads and other buildings, such as St Andrew's Cathedral *(see page 23)*. Since 1950 it has been necessary to introduce tighter immigration laws to stem the tide of migrants from the subcontinent.

That the various ethnic groups and cultures have been able to work together is partly the result of the government's authoritarian leadership style. The private life of the citizens is subject to countless regulations and governmental advice. In 1987 the Ministry of Health started a campaign to increase the birth rate, but they did not want to leave the matter of the next generation's intelligence to chance and the officials spoke of the need for children from the educated elite. The daily newspaper, the *Straits Times*, once commissioned an opinion poll to find out why Singaporeans were not interested in literature. The answer came back: 'They expect me to flush the toilet, to walk along Orchard Road, not to go into the city centre during the rush hour, to look after my wife and have a family. And now they want me to find time to read books!'

But Singaporeans rarely respond angrily to the government's constant urgings towards self-improvement. Basically, everyone goes along with what those in power ordain – and they will probably continue to do so, as long as their material welfare remains secure. Striving for material gain and success is deeply ingrained in the Chinese psyche, although recently this approach has lost favour with the ruling class. Shortly before his resignation, the long-serving prime minister Lee Kuan Yew condemned 'materialism without morals'. He invoked the basic values of Confucianism, namely that the individual is subordinate to the needs of the wider community. Prosperity, therefore, is not equated with the selfish free-for-all that is often the consequence of pure capitalism.

At the moment there are fewer females than males.

A happy couple

Nearly half of all women work and make a considerable contribution to the family income; the top and well-paid jobs are still filled predominantly by men, however. Compared with other Asian countries, the Singaporean standard of living is relatively high. The average monthly income is S$2,500, a healthy figure by any standards. But given rising costs of living, including astronomical prices for cars and private houses, it is a sum that does not go very far in Singapore.

Housing

Despite the construction of huge apartment blocks in the suburbs, living space is still in short supply, so, often against their will, young people are obliged to live with their parents. Only married couples and singles over the age of 35 are granted flats by the Housing Development Board. Home for almost 90 percent of Singaporeans is a flat in a multi-storey block. The state has introduced a form of compulsory saving, the Central Provident Fund, towards home ownership: a part of a worker's wages is set aside, not just for a pension scheme but also for the purchase of a home. A three-bedroom flat in the suburbs, leased for 99 years, costs between S$130,000 and S$150,000. The door behind the surrounding balcony, which is often visible from ground level, will probably reveal the race of the owner. The Chinese often have a red pelmet stretched out above the door as a good luck symbol, Indians place a few lemon tree branches behind the door frame, while the Malays invariably leave their prayer mat hanging to air over the railings.

Religion

Religious freedom exists in Singapore. Most Chinese are Buddhists, Confucians or Taoists or else they take a little from all three. Chinese temples are dedicated to a hotchpotch of saints who are worshipped when required. *Nirvana*, a state of blessedness in which all human desire is extinguished, is the ultimate goal for Buddhists. To reach this exalted state and achieve release from the cycle of birth and rebirth, it is necessary to lead a life full of good deeds. Everyone's fate rests in their own hands, as the quality of the next life depends on how the individual has behaved in his or her life.

Confucianism emphasises adherence to a set of moral values, that require the individual to bow to the wishes of the community. Taoism is also linked with Buddhism, but here, man is subjected to the will of nature. Life should follow its 'natural' course, in harmony and moderation and with modesty and meditation.

Most Malays are Moslems. Islam was brought to the region in the 12th century by merchants from India and

Subsidised housing

11

Worship at the temple

Sultan Mosque and Hindu deity at the Sri Mariammen Temple

Arabia. According to the teachings of the prophet Mohammed, there is only one God, Allah. Every practising Moslem should pray to Allah five times each day, observe the fasting month of Ramadan and make a pilgrimage to Mecca once during his lifetime. Although the religious life of the Moslem community takes place away from the public gaze, the impact of Islam in Singapore is considerable.

Most Indians are Hindus. The numerous Hindu gods are all manifestations of one god, the spirit Brahman, to whom everyone's being is subordinate. Like Buddhists, Hindus believe in rebirth. There are a number of ways to escape from this cycle: one way is through a life of asceticism and meditation; another way lies through good deeds, pilgrimages and an exemplary way of life. The caste system, an important element in Hindu society elsewhere, is not adhered to in modern Singapore.

Constitution and politics

When Singapore gained partial independence in 1959, the new state adopted a British-style parliamentary system. The president is the republic's head of state and he or she is elected by the people for a period of six years. In consultation with the party that commands a parliamentary majority, the president will appoint the prime minister and also the cabinet. The single-chamber parliament, the National Assembly, consists of 83 Members of Parliament (MPs) who are elected into office every five years. All Singaporeans aged 21 or over are entitled to vote.

The PAP (People's Action Party) has been the majority party in parliament since independence. Opposition parties such as the SDP (Singapore Democratic Party) and the Workers' Party have gradually increased their share of the vote, but, as minority parties, they have no real power. Lee Kuan Yew was Singapore's prime minister for 31 years and was responsible for the city-state's post-independence history.

In 1963, he achieved his first major political victory: Malaya and Singapore combined to form the Malaysian Federation. The British feared that the abandoned trading post would not survive without a hinterland, so union with Malaya was perceived as a sensible solution. However, racial and political differences between the economically superior Chinese and politically strong Malays on both sides of the Causeway soon shattered any dreams of a united Malaysian nationhood. In 1965 Singapore left the Federation and became an independent republic.

Since 1990 the government has been led by Goh Chok Tong, who was groomed for the job by his predecessor. But his hold on power cannot easily be compared with that of Lee Kuan Yew, who still has a say in the running of the party, as does his influential son Lee Hsien Loong. Maintaining internal security and social and political stability are still important aims; some Western critics believe that too much emphasis is placed on these policies.

Singapore united

Officially there is press freedom, but local publications are not known for departing conspicuously from the government line. The same is true of foreign newspapers and magazines, whose criticisms are condemned as an uninformed and unwarranted interference in Singapore's internal affairs. In 1994, for example, the government took libel action against the *International Herald Tribune* after an article spoke of 'the compliant justice system of some Asian countries'. The writer, an American professor at a Singapore university, soon found himself on his way back to the US.

13

And yet it would be wrong to describe Singapore as a police state. There is no secret police. Singapore is a democracy, but one in which the underlying political and social assumptions have not been seriously questioned by a significant number of people. Censors ensure no pornographic material reaches the island. Prostitution is not forbidden, but it is not officially recognised. Brothels exist only in certain streets and are strictly controlled. After a further tightening up of the drugs law, 'incurable addicts' face canings and imprisonment. Drug dealers, like murderers, can expect a death sentence if convicted.

Local laws

Practically every souvenir shop in Singapore sells white T-shirts printed with the warning of a fine for not flushing the toilet. Such fines are a serious matter for Singaporeans. Although in practice no one has ever been fined for not flushing, draconian punishments can be meted out without hesitation. The police are conspicuous, and it's no accident that Singapore ranks as one of the world's

More symbols of the city

Freighters at the container port

safest countries. However, one does not have to be a hardened criminal to fall foul of the law. Improper behaviour, such as dropping litter, is enough and, throwing chewing gum on the pavement or road can result in a S$500 fine. To reinforce this law, the import and export of chewing gum is forbidden, although Singaporeans can bring in a small amount for personal consumption. The laws about smoking in public places are likewise very strict.

Economy

The city-state of Singapore has one of the highest living standards in Asia; indeed it is among the 20 wealthiest countries in the world. 'Be the best that we can be' is a frequent battle-cry and just one of the slogans that the government uses in its campaigns to spur on the people. In 1996 Singapore lost its status in the OECD as a 'developing nation'. During the 1980s, economic growth was always above 9 percent per annum. Although this rate slowed during the 1985–87 recession, since 1994 it has been gradually rising again. However, the economic downturn which affected Asia in 1997 has taken its toll in Singapore. Although it registered a dismal 1.5 percent growth in 1998, it rebounded strongly to a 5 percent increase in 1999 due to cost-cutting measures taken to enhance competitiveness, economic restructuring and a S$10.5-billion stimulus package to kickstart the economy.

With no hinterland, no raw materials, no agricultural land, not even enough water to satisfy its own requirements (a pipeline from Malaysia keeps the taps running), the Singapore government had to come up with something special to provide a decent living for its people. One of the most important early decisions was to expand the port facilities, and the harbour is now one of the biggest and busiest in the world. Round the clock, freighters are loaded

Open-air dining

and unloaded in the ultra-modern, electronically-controlled container port. Tankers from Brunei, Malaysia, Indonesia and the Middle East supply oil to the massive refinery. Singapore's shipyards are among the most up-to-date in the world and cruise ships moor at a specially-built terminal. At the hub of the international air travel network, Singapore's Changi airport is another showpiece. Passenger records are broken every year and Singapore Airlines has a reputation as one of the world's most modern airlines. In 1998 Singapore welcomed 6 million tourists.

Immediately after the republic was founded, the government put the economy on an upward trend, as industry was transformed. Out went labour-intensive, low-profit trades such as textiles, in came companies specialising in high-value-added technologies such as communications and electronics. Incentives were given to foreign investors, as the government soon recognised the advantages of international capital. Only China has attracted more foreign investment in recent years. Many multinational companies have offices in the city and the foreign exchange market is of vital importance to the region. The turnover of the 90 or so banks that deal in foreign currencies exceeds that of their rivals in Hong Kong, and Singaporean traders have a reputation for integrity in financial dealing. Since the Asian crisis, economic restructuring has gathered pace. The financial sector was liberalised with more full-bank licences issued to foreign banks. Numerous foreign mutual fund managers came to tap what is generally agreed as a multi-billion dollar industry. In 2000, the lucrative telecommunications market was deregulated to attract more players to make Singapore an Asian communications hub.

High-rise developments

15

Cottage industries

Many of the city's traditional crafts are hanging on grimly. The cottage industries that make masks for Chinese festivals, flower garlands for Indian temple visitors and incense candles for Buddhists are usually run from tiny, dark, ground-floor rooms in old Singapore. Basket-makers remain in Arab Street, goldsmiths in Little India and noodle manufacturers in Chinatown and their produce is often sold at the door beneath the narrow arcade known as the 'five foot way', the local term for the five-foot wide pavement.

Flower garlands

One of the reasons for the cottage industry decline is that skilled craftsmen can scarcely afford the ever-increasing rents in houses that are gradually undergoing restoration. The next generation is also unwilling to take over these trades, where skills have traditionally been handed down from father to son. Ambitious young Singaporeans see no future in eking out a meagre existence seven days a week from a tiny workshop.

Historical Highlights

Historians cannot agree on the first mention of Singapore, but it is said that the Chinese gave the name Pu-luo-chung to the island in the 3rd century AD. In 1330 a small settlement was discovered by a Chinese explorer named Pancur. Singapore, often called Temasek in the literature of that period, was probably founded around the middle of the 13th century by the Sri Vijaya empire in Sumatra.

14–18th century First Siam (now Thailand), then Java (the Majapahit empire) seize the small island but show little interest in it. At the beginning of the 16th century, the Portuguese capture Malacca, then an important centre in East-West trade. In the 17th century, the island of Singapore is settled by about 100 Orang Lauts or sea nomads. At the end of the 18th century, the British and the 'British East India Company' open a trading post in Penang and take Malacca from the Dutch, who dominate the region at the time.

1819 On 29 January, Stamford Raffles (Governor of Bencoolen, West Sumatra) arrives in Singapore and the next day, with the help of the Sultan of Johor Riau (the southernmost province of Malaya) and the Temenggong, his representative on the island, opens a trading post for the East India Comany to deal with maritime traffic between China and India.

1824 The British agree to withdraw from Indonesia, in return for which the Dutch recognise British rights over Singapore. The Sultan cedes Singapore in perpetuity to the British.

1826 The trading stations at Penang, Malacca and Singapore are named the 'Straits Settlements', under the control of British India.

1867 On 1 April Singapore becomes a British Crown Colony, controlled by the Colonial Office in London. The population stands at 80,000, most of them Chinese.

End of the 19th century The Suez Canal opens and the number of ships calling in at Singapore increases. Trade flourishes. Henry Ridley, director of the Botanic Gardens in Singapore, succeeds in growing a rubber tree. The Malaysian peninsula and Singapore develop into the world's main rubber producers. In 1888 John Dunlop invents the rubber tyre.

1923 Singapore is linked to Malaysia by a causeway.

1942 The Japanese, led by General Tomoyuki Yamashita, invade and occupy Singapore.

1945–48 The Allies defeat the Japanese in the Far East. Singapore reverts to Crown Colony status.

1955 The Rendel Constitution granted by the British leads to elections and David Marshall becomes chief minister. A legislative council consisting of 32 members, 25 of whom are elected, is established. The Labour Front have a majority, but the PAP (People's Action Party) forms a powerful opposition.

1956 After failing to negotiate complete independence from the Crown, Marshall resigns and is replaced as chief minister by Lim Yew Hock.

1958 A constitutional agreement for partial independence for Singapore is finally signed in London, providing for a fully elected legislative assembly, which, however, would have no power over external affairs and no absolute control of an internal security council.

1959 The first general election for the fully legislative assembly results in Lee Kuan Yew becoming prime minister as leader of the victorious PAP, which wins an absolute majority (43 out 51 seats – with 53 percent of the popular vote).

1963 The people of Malaya, Sarawak, North Borneo (now Sabah) and Singapore vote to form the Federation of Malaysia.

1965 Singapore leaves the Federation of Malaysia and becomes an independent sovereign nation, a member of both the United Nations and the Commonwealth.

1967 Singapore, Malaysia, Thailand, Indonesia, the Philippines and Brunei form a political and economic union known as the ASEAN (Association of Southeast Asian Nations).

1968 In the general election the PAP wins all 58 seats.

1970–89 The PAP continues to dominate parliament, but at the start of the 1980s, Lee Kuan Yew's party has to live with an opposition party.

1981 In a by-election, J.B. Jeyaratnam of the Workers' Party wins the first seat to be held by an opposition member.

1990 Lee Kuan Yew retires as prime minister and is replaced by Goh Chok Tong.

1993 Ong Teng Cheong becomes the first elected president in Singapore.

1998 Second Link, the new bridge to Malaysia, opens at Tuas.

1999 Government proposes measures to keep the economy competitive. Former Ambassador-at-Large, S.R. Nathan returns unopposed as the second elected president.

Sir Stamford Raffles

Thomas Stamford Bingley Raffles was born at sea off the coast of Jamaica on 6 July 1781. At the age of 15 he found work as an official with the East India Company, and while exploring the Southeast Asia coast for new trading outlets, he discovered the temple city of Borobudur in Java (for which he was knighted).

He was not favoured by the ruling Conservatives but still won an important place in the pantheon of British colonialists by developing Singapore into a flourishing trading post. He got rid of the island's rats by paying a cash sum for every dead rat, and prevented racial conflict by settling the various ethnic groups into separate quarters. Chinatown, Little India and the Arab Street district owe their character to Raffles. His own residence was built on the present fort at Canning Hill, where he felt that the fresh sea breeze was beneficial to his fragile health.

Raffles' private life was far from happy. His first wife died shortly after their marriage and all four children from his second marriage perished at an early age, three of malaria. Raffles himself died just one day before his 45th birthday. Even the flower that was named after him does not do him justice. Rafflesia is a parasitic plant that smells of putrid meat.

Lee Kuan Yew

When, on 16 September 1923, a boy by the name of Lee Kuan Yew was born into a wealthy Chinese family, no one imagined that he would one day lead the island's government and become a world-respected statesman. However, the boy's parents were clearly not without ambition for their bright son, as they also called him Harry and had him educated according to the English model, something that would surely be of benefit to his professional career, given the circumstances of colonial rule.

He went to grammar school and studied at Raffles College. In September 1946, one year after the Japanese surrender, Harry Lee Kuan Yew, then aged 23, went to Cambridge to study law. He gained a double first and was admitted to the English bar in 1950. That same year he met his future wife, Kwa Geok Choo, who had also studied at Cambridge. Instead of practising as a barrister in England, he returned to Singapore, where he was appointed legal adviser to the Postal Union. He began learning Mandarin and became politically active, joining like-minded young professionals to campaign for an end to British rule on the island.

The People's Action Party (PAP) was founded with Lee Kuan Yew as its general secretary. Even though at times Lee co-operated with some of the more radical opponents of British colonial rule, namely the Communist Party, he was always a fanatical anti-communist. In 1958, Lee helped to negotiate for Singapore the status of self-governing state within the British Commonwealth. Elections were held in May 1959, with Lee campaigning on an anti-colonialist, anti-communist platform. On 5 June, the newly elected Prime Minister Lee Kuan Yew announced that he and his ministers had taken over the running of all internal affairs. The English yoke had finally been shaken off.

Some refer to him respectfully as 'Mr Singapore', others less deferentially, but still affectionately, as 'Uncle Harry'. The Chinese liked to describe him as a banana: yellow on the outside, white on the inside. Nevertheless, his self-discipline and successful battle against corruption remain an example to other rulers. Singapore without Lee Kuan Yew seems impossible to imagine. What about Lee Kuan Yew without Singapore? He was once asked whether he regarded himself as Chinese: 'Ethnically, I am certainly Chinese, but otherwise I am a Singaporean'.

Route 1

On the trail of Raffles – the Colonial District

To fully appreciate this tour of Singapore's colonial past – the Civic and Cultural District – visitors will need a whole day. In the heart of the modern city stand impressive monuments from the 19th century which testify to the prosperity of the former British trading post. Alongside the towering steel and glass office blocks, some of which reach a height of 280m (920ft), the grandiose colonial-style architecture looks modest but nevertheless solid. An ascent of one of the skyscrapers, included in the route, provides a magnificent panoramic view of much of Singapore. To fit in a tour of the Singapore History Museum, set out in good time, preferably by 9am.

Raffles Place

Raffles Place is a small, green oasis set between the huge office blocks of the Central Business District on the Singapore River's southern bank. Passers-by often take a break on the square's neatly trimmed lawn while, underneath, lies the cavernous Raffles Place underground station, one of the busiest on the network.

To the west, the rectangular square is bordered by the soaring 280-m (920-ft) **OUB Centre ❶**, designed by the well-known Japanese architect, Kenzo Tange. Tange also designed the equally impressive and newer ★★ **UOB Plaza**, which is exactly the same height and offers stunning views from the expensive Chinese restaurant on the 60th floor (**Top of the Plaza**, tel: 538 3232). However, not everyone can afford the staggering prices, so for a free view of the northern side of the city, take the first lift (from the second floor) to the 38th floor **Sky Lobby**. The triumvirate of massive skyscrapers in the area is completed by the **Republic Plaza** just across at Market Street, with its striking blue facade (also 280m/920ft high).

A panoramic view of Singapore is also available for free on the other side of Chulia Street by the banks of the Singapore River.

Follow the river downstream as far as **Cavenagh Bridge**. To the right of this iron suspension bridge (completed in 1869) is the enormous **Fullerton Building**. Built by the British in 1928 as the General Post Office, a function it continued to perform until the late 1990s. It is due to re-open in 2001 as the luxury Grand Fullerton Hotel.

Cavenagh Bridge

On the other side of the bridge, it is impossible to miss the palatial ★ **Empress Place Building ❷** that dates from 1854. It was used first as the courthouse and then as offices for the emigration and immigration authorities. It was rather half-heartedly restored in 1989 to house a museum for Asian cultures, only to close again in 1995. In 2001, the building will re-open as the second wing of the Asian Civilisations Museum which is on Armenian Street (*see page 25*). The new museum will have four galleries devoted to 'China', 'Southeast Asia', 'Islamic' and 'India'. One thing that certainly will not be open to the public is the mysterious **time capsule**, which is kept beneath a glass pyramid outside the entrance. It is due to be opened in 2015 when Singapore celebrates 50 years of independence.

The mysterious time capsule

21

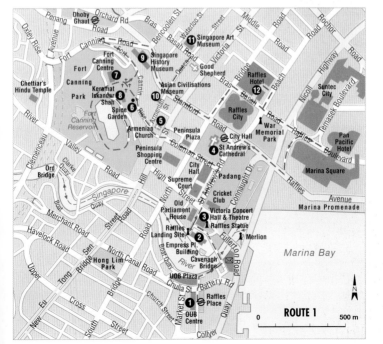

ROUTE 1

0   500 m

Parliament House

A few yards from the riverbank stands a tall white **obelisk** which was built by the colonial rulers during 1850 in honour of the Indian governor, Dalhousie. It marks the start of a pretty avenue which leads directly to the dark, bronze **Raffles Statue**. Unveiled in 1887, the sculpture is just one of the many tributes to the founder of Singapore. It is set against the backdrop of the **Victoria Concert Hall and Theatre ❸**, the home of the Singapore Symphony Orchestra. The Concert Hall is the island's premier venue for opera, ballet and classical music, while the Victoria Theatre is a showcase for plays, both local and imported.

Follow the narrow lane that passes to the left of the concert hall as far as Parliament Lane. This leads directly up to the old **Parliament House** (1827), whose iron gate conceals huge, light-grey stone columns. It was planned by architect George Coleman, who was responsible for several of Singapore's notable buildings. This structure served as a debating chamber from the 1950s until September 1999 when New Parliament House, just next door, was completed. It is five times larger than the old building but still retains the colonial architectural style.

Skyscrapers dominate Boat Quay
Raffles Landing Site

Another ★ **statue** of Sir Stamford Raffles stands at the point where Parliament Lane meets the bank of the Singapore River, but this one is gleaming white. This spot is known as the **Raffles Landing Site** as it was here on 29 January 1819 that the city's founder first set foot on Singaporean soil. On the opposite side of the river lies the ★★ **Boat Quay**, a complex with many restaurants and bars which was restored during the 1980s. The run-down stores and tiny ground-floor workshops were once home to more rats than people. Now the pulsating nightlife goes on until the early hours.

For a fascinating excursion along the ★★ **Singapore River**, take one of the so-called *bumboats* which depart

from the Landing Site (daily 9am–10pm; departs when there are 12 passengers waiting). The boat trips first head upstream beneath the low bridges as far as the **Ord Bridge**, where there was once a Malay village. They then turn round and sail down to the mouth of the river where the symbol of Singapore, the half-lion, half-fish ★ **Merlion** *(see page 5)*, a popular subject for amateur photographers, is situated. The recorded commentary describes in detail the history of the trading post. It also explains the original function of the wooden *bumboats* – they were employed to carry goods from the vessels anchored in the harbour to the warehouses further upriver. Mention is also made of how the quality of the water has changed: the river was once a foul-smelling sewer.

Merlion – half-lion, half-fish

Go back down Parliament Lane to High Street. About 10m (11 yds) further on to the left, before the narrow north front of the old Parliament House, a black **miniature elephant** with white tusks stands on a stone plinth. This fine-looking statue was a gift to Singapore from the King of Siam during an official visit on 16 March 1871. Diagonally opposite the statue lies the **Padang**, or 'field' in Malay. In the colonial era, sports, games, military parades and social events were held here. This grassy area, the size of several football pitches, is still used for public occasions, including the annual celebration of the country's independence. Take a good look at the **Singapore Cricket Club** clubhouse. This building (1852) that houses the elite club is a fine example of the colonial architectural style found throughout the tropics. The faded charm within can only be imagined, as it is closed to tourists. At the north end of the Padang is one of Singapore's oldest leisure clubs, the **Singapore Recreation Club**, recently rebuilt on its original site.

Several splendid edifices can be seen on the other side of **St Andrew's Road**. As public buildings, they are open to visitors. The first is the ★ **Supreme Court**. This classical building with a facade of stout Corinthian columns projects a sense of dignity. Dating from 1939, it is one of the last colonial constructions built in the city. Only a little older but no less impressive is the huge flight of steps beneath the colonnade of the next monumental structure: the ★ **City Hall**. Finished in 1929, it was the setting for the public surrender of the Japanese after World War II.

The Supreme Court

Built in 1863, the gleaming white ★ **St Andrew's Cathedral** ❹ is a major landmark. The biggest church in Singapore, its interior is modestly decorated, whitewashed walls and a few stained-glass windows behind the altar. It is, nevertheless, ideal not only for quiet contemplation but also as a cool refuge from the tropical heat.

St Andrew's Cathedral

Coleman Street, named after the creative and highly regarded architect George Coleman, leads into the heart

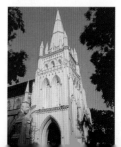

of one of the city's shopping quarters. On the right is the **Peninsula Plaza**, on the left the **Peninsula Shopping Centre**; and there are a number of places nearby to enjoy a fortifying drink before starting out on the arduous climb that lies ahead.

First cross the broad Hill Street and enter the pleasantly cool **Armenian Church of St Gregory ❺**. This small, apostolic chapel (1835), with a roof constructed by Coleman, is the oldest church in Singapore. As the Armenian community has declined, services rarely take place in this simple, sacred building.

Coleman Street now climbs gently and becomes the steeper Canning Rise which winds its way up ★★ **Fort Canning Hill**. Behind the Registry of Marriages lies **Fort Canning Park**, with its large areas of well-tended grass. Just to the right is the **Spice Garden ❻** and it is worth stopping here for a few minutes to enjoy the scents. This is a miniature version of the 19-hectare (47-acre) garden that Raffles laid out in 1822 on what was then Government Hill. He wanted to find out which spices grew well in the tropical heat of Singapore. Many, such as cloves and nutmeg, thrived. These discoveries brought riches to Singapore until the middle of the 19th century. Exotic spices were as precious as gold, and every European maritime power sought to gain control over this profitable trade.

Entrance to the Spice Garden

Cross the Spice Garden and pass through the weathered, stone arch to the **Christian cemetery** with its 600 or so graves. The gravestones have been bedded into the perimeter wall. Although the inscriptions are difficult to read, they describe the tragic fate that befell many Chinese and European Christians who were buried here during the 19th century. The name of architect Coleman appears once again: his tombstone shows the year of his death as 1841.

Fort Canning Centre

A stone staircase leads up to the **Fort Canning Centre ❼**, where the **Singapore Dance Theatre** trains and rehearses. Another flight of stairs behind the building leads up to the sparse remains of **Fort Canning**. It was built by the British between 1859 and 1861 as a fortification and consists of an arms store, hospital and barracks. Its construction involved levelling off an area of about 3 hectares (7 acres) at the summit. However, the thick walls were demolished in 1926 and, apart from an old stone gate, there is little to see. Enjoy a few minutes of peace in the shadow of some large fig trees. Only cheerful birdsong and the screeching of cicadas interrupt the silence.

A well-signposted circular tour branches off at the old stone gate to the higher **Fort Canning Reservoir**, which affords some attractive views over the city. The path passes some historic plaques and ancient, iron cannons – but none of them originated from the old fort. Just before the path arrives back at the Fort Canning Centre, on the hillside

to the right, lies the **Keramat Iskandar Shah** , a richly decorated tombstone. The Malays still honour Sultan Megat Iskandar Shah, who founded Melaka at the beginning of the 15th century. For Malays, the hill is sacred. They call it the **Forbidden Hill**, but Raffles disregarded their feelings.

A well-earned break

Descend through the Christian cemetery and then pass through the left-hand stone arch. Fort Canning Rise leads to Fort Canning Road. The ★★ **Singapore History Museum** ❾ (Tues–Sun 9am–5.30pm; nearest MRT station: Dhoby Ghaut) is situated to the right at the junction with Stamford Road. Built in 1887 in classical style, the building, with its green shutters, resembles an official residence. It contains many items relating to the history, ethnology and archaeology of Southeast Asia, and Singapore in particular. A full tour will take at least an hour and a half.

Continue along Stamford Road past the red-brick National Library, which may in the near future disappear from the landscape to make way for a new tunnel and the proposed city campus of the Singapore Management University, due to open in 2002.

The trishaw alternative

The **National Museum Shop** *(see Shopping, page 81)* at No 51 Armenian Street can be reached by taking a short detour to the right. This store sells attractive souvenirs and informative books on the history of Singapore. On the same street at No 39 is the ★★ **Asian Civilisations Museum** ❿ (Tues–Sun 9am–5.30pm; Wed till 9pm) which showcases Asian cultures and civilisations with themed displays of artefacts and exciting multimedia programmes.

A detour to the left into Queen Street leads to the impressive stone **Cathedral of the Good Shepherd**. Designed by Dennis McSwiney, a pupil of George Coleman, it was completed in 1846. Opposite, the ★★ **Singapore Art Museum** ⓫ (Tues–Sun 9am–5.30pm) occupies what was St Joseph's Institution, a mission school founded by

View from the Westin Stamford

Raffles Hotel

Poolside at the Marina Mandarin

the French De La Salle Order in 1867. Contemporary art from Southeast Asia is now displayed here.

Return to Stamford Road. Look for the designer clothes displayed in several small but unusual boutiques. Diagonally opposite (and impossible to miss) is the gleaming, silver shopping palace known as **Raffles City**. To cool down and relax, make for this elegant air-conditioned complex with its two hotels. One of Singapore's most-photographed prospects can be enjoyed from the expensive ★ **Compass Rose** restaurant in the **Westin Stamford Hotel**. The view is not quite so impressive from the bar, also on the 70th floor (218m/715ft) – hence the cheaper prices. It is possible to look down into War Memorial Park on the other side of Beach Road where a monument known as **Chopsticks** honours those who fell in World War II.

Leave Raffles City by the Bras Basah Road exit, cross the road and there stands the gleaming white ★★★ **Raffles Hotel ⑫**. When examined at close quarters, the walls clearly do not date from the colonial era. This luxurious hotel was re-opened in 1991 after two years of comprehensive renovation and the addition of new annexes. It all started in 1887 when two Armenian brothers, the Sarkies, converted a few rooms into a simple hotel. Now the guests stay in grand suites and non-residents swell the crowds attracted to the hotel by the two-storey arcade with its array of expensive boutiques, jewellers, art dealers, designers, top-class restaurants and bars *(see Food and Drink, page 77)*. Non-residents may enter the hotel, but access to the guests' lounges is not permitted – it is only possible to look in from the outside. The atmosphere in the famous "Grand Old Lady of the East", as the wealthy 19th-century travellers called it, can be sampled in the reception hall (entrance in Beach Road). Follow Rudyard Kipling's example and enjoy a Singapore Sling *(see page 77)* in the Long Bar.

Leave the hotel by the main entrance, turn right and follow Beach Road. At the next junction turn left into Raffles Boulevard. On the left-hand side stands **Suntec City**, housing five office tower blocks, a convention hall and Singapore's largest shopping centre (Suntec City Mall). More shopping can be had at Marina Square with its four hotels: The **Marina Mandarin** has the biggest atrium in Southeast Asia and the **Pan Pacific** has a glass lift, from which diners can survey the city as they rise to the **Hai Tien Lo** restaurant. **Esplanade Park**, between Marina Square and Marina Bay, is currently being converted into the **Esplanade-Theatres on the Bay**, due to open in 2002. The complex will have a 1,800-seat concert hall, a 2,000-seat theatre, an outdoor amphitheatre and numerous eating outlets. The famous **Satay Club** will also re-open. The City Hall MRT station is only a short distance away.

Route 2

Orchard Road

The Singaporeans' enthusiasm for shopping is encapsulated in the expression 'Shop 'til you drop'. At some time or other, everyone will probably feel like dropping when on a shopping excursion through the multi-storey malls of Orchard Road: it may be fatigue or it may be the prices that the international designers and couturiers command. Orchard Road is no place for bargain hunters, but window shoppers will enjoy the stylish displays. Despite the vastness of the shopping areas, the range of merchandise is less wide than one might imagine.

Shoppers will certainly not succumb to the heat, as the stores are all air-conditioned – sometimes the temperature controls are set just a little too low. Well-stocked food stalls and supermarkets in the basements will take care of any hunger pangs.

Shop 'til you drop

The Orchard Road shops start on a fairly modest scale by the **Dhoby Ghaut** MRT station. On the left-hand side by Penang Road lies **Park Mall**, which houses more than 45 shops specialising in furnishings, appliances and fixtures for every room in the house. The 1960s **Plaza Singapura** ⓭ has been given a new lease of life after recent rebuilding and refurbishment. Its principal tenants are the Daimaru department store, Courts and Yamaha Music School.

Follow the right-hand side of Orchard Road past the well-protected entrance to **Istana**, the president's palace. The palace lies in parkland, hidden away behind thick vegetation, and the neatly dressed guards will not allow unauthorised visitors on to the site.

27

The malls are multi-storey

A few yards further down the road in the basement of the **Le Meridien Hotel**, the former Duty Free Shop (DFS) used to attract Japanese tour groups but is now home to the gigantic **Kopitiam Food Court**. It is a good place to stop for some tea and snacks while watching the human traffic on Orchard Road.

There is nothing fashionable about **Orchard Plaza** ⓮, but to compensate, the prices in these overflowing souvenir, shoe and textile shops are very reasonable. The Goh Kin Camera Service on the 2nd floor provides a rapid camera repair service.

The **Singapore Post Philatelic Bureau** on the other side of the busy road is great for stamp collectors (*see Shopping, pages 81*).

Continue on the right-hand side of Orchard Road and **Orchard Point** ⓯ is the next shopping centre. The four-storey building is modern and spacious inside. Some interesting antique shops can be found on the top floor.

Back outside amid the hurly-burly of hurrying shoppers, take a right turn into **Cuppage Road**. This quickly leads to ★ **Cuppage Terrace** (*see Nightlife, page 82*), a busy square surrounded by bars, restaurants and snack food outlets. This is a favourite haunt of Singapore's large expatriate community.

Centrepoint

One of the busiest and most attractive shopping centres is **Centrepoint** ⓰. The tastefully decorated shops of famous fashion designers are spread over four floors. But other, more affordable stores such as Marks & Spencer and Robinsons are also here. Large bookshops such as **Times The Bookshop** stock a good range of international and Singaporean literature. The **Marketplace** is a convenient stop for meals.

Peranakan Place

★★ **Peranakan Place**, a little further on, is also very popular with tourists. On the one hand, it is possible to

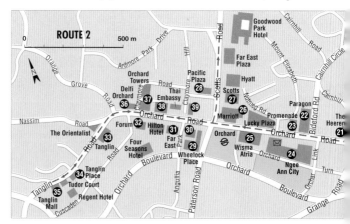

ROUTE 2

watch the hustle and bustle of Orchard Road over a beer in one of the street cafés, on the other, it is one way of getting to know Peranakan architecture (*see page 9*).

Follow ★ **Emerald Hill Road** ⑰ uphill for a short distance, looking out for the extravagantly restored, two-storey dwellings of the old Peranakan population. Many have now been converted into agencies, offices and restaurants.

Several sports clothing shops and a number of well-stocked watch and clock shops, specialising in the colourful Swatch brands, can be found in the adjoining **Orchard Emerald Shopping Centre** ⑱.

The **John Little** department store in the **Specialist's Shopping Centre** ⑲ on the other side of Orchard Road is renowned, among other things, for its large selection of fabrics.

Several multi-storey shops now follow closely on the right-hand side of the road. There is the rather charmless **Midpoint Orchard** and then **Orchard Shopping Centre**. The exquisite fashion outlets of **OG Orchard** ⑳ deserve a closer examination. Also worth exploring is the five-storey shoppers' paradise **The Heeren** ㉑, which houses HMV, the largest CD shop here.

Expensive, international fashion designer outlets are housed strictly according to status in the smart **Paragon Shopping Centre** ㉒. At the very top is the **Metro** department store, while in the basement the **Sogo** chain has established a lavishly stocked supermarket. Freshly prepared and reasonably priced *sushi* are among its attractions.

In the **Promenade Shopping Centre** ㉓, the elegant and creative displays (principally the work of young Asian fashion designers) can be seen from a walkway that ascends in a spiral.

Emerald Hill facades

29

Vintage models on display

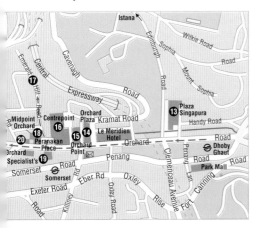

Ngee Ann City

Goodwood Park Hotel

Wheelock Place

On the other side of the street, the ★★ **Ngee Ann City** ㉔ is an even larger and smarter shopping citadel. The two towers are occupied, both above and below ground, by 130 speciality shops. Other large department stores such as **Takashimaya** and **Harrods** are based here. Look out for the shop that sells souvenirs of the Eastern & Oriental Express and Kinokuniya Bookshop, the largest in Singapore, while Basement B2 is paradise for gourmets. A post office is located on the fourth floor, while on the fifth level is the Library@Orchard, a lifestyle library catering to young people.

The facade of the adjacent **Wisma Atria** ㉕ looks rather modest by comparison, but the interior consists of neat galleries with small and attractive fashion boutiques. It also houses the Japanese **Isetan** department store with its wide range of merchandise. In the basement near the entrance to Orchard MRT station, a subway leads under the road towards Scotts Road and **Tangs** ㉖, Singapore's busiest department store famous for its bargain sales.

Next door is the once popular **Lucky Plaza**. Many of the traders have given up trying to entice tourists into their photography, luggage and jewellery shops by claiming huge price reductions. Haggling is perfectly acceptable here, but shoppers should be wary, as there are some unscrupulous traders about.

A detour along Scotts Road passes some of the city's finest hotels (Marriott, Hyatt, etc). More elegant shopping centres lie beyond. In **Scotts** ㉗, for example, the shops specialise in cosmetics and fashions for young people.

Ready for a drink? On the right-hand side, just a few yards further on, is the ★★ **Goodwood Park Hotel**, formerly known as the 'Teutonia Club', the meeting place for the German community before World War I. 'High tea' which consists of a wide selection of sandwiches and cakes is available in L'Espresso between 2.30 and 6.30pm.

Pacific Plaza ㉘ is another attractive shopping centre. Take a look at the huge selection of CDs in **Tower Records** on the top floor. Just next door is **Shaw Centre**, a shopping mall cum cineplex and home to another **Isetan** department store.

Return to the junction with Orchard Road and cross over to the huge glass complex **Wheelock Place** ㉙. Inside, you'll find **Marks and Spencer** with its range of quality clothes and foods occupying the two basement levels, while on the ground floor is **Borders**, the giant American bookstore chain.

At **Liat Towers** ㉚ you can't miss Planet Hollywood, the exclusive Hermes boutique, Starbucks and Esprit boutique. **The Far East Shopping Centre** ㉛ with its narrow walkways and little shops is one of Singapore's older shopping centres. Tailors offer their services with typical

Oriental aplomb, but there are also jewellers, opticians, camera shops and antique sellers.

The next building combines the **Hilton Hotel** and a shopping arcade – filled with designer-brand shops and world-class jewellers like Cartier and Bvlgari – that leads through to Orchard Boulevard and the **Four Seasons** hotel. With numerous children's clothes shops and a multinational toy chain, **Forum the Shopping Mall** ❷ has set its sights firmly on the younger generation, but there are also one or two fine fashion boutiques for adults.

Forum

On the left-hand side, where Orchard Road becomes **Tanglin Road**, the **Tanglin Shopping Centre** ❸ recently underwent a facelift and lost some of its special atmosphere in the process, but it is still renowned for its made-to-measure tailoring. The **China Silk House** on level 2 has a wide selection of flowing Chinese silks. Also noteworthy are the shops specialising in exquisite Persian, Pakistani and Afghan rugs and carpets; the fine arts and antique shops like Antiques of the Orient; and CT Hoo which sells Mikimoto pearls from Japan.

Fashionable accessories

31

Tastefully imitating the English country house style is **Tanglin Place** ❹. The charming **Tudor Court** next door is attractive, and trendy **Tanglin Mall** ❺ ahead houses a good mixture of outlets selling everything from comics to ethnic collectibles, plus a supermarket.

Return to Scotts Road on the other side of Tanglin Road where the mammoth **Orientalists** carpet store is located. Inside is an amazing collection of hand-knotted carpets in both traditional and modern designs. The white-tiled facade of the **Delfi Orchard** ❻ gleams brightly at the junction with Orchard Road. Chrome and glass cannot conceal the fact that many of the spaces are vacant. In the merciless fight for custom, this shopping mall has been on the losing side. Between the gaps, a few bridal boutiques and kitchen shops have survived.

Orchard Towers ❼ is different. The appetising smells emanating from the food stalls in the basement attract scores of shoppers. **Miss Ming** on the first floor sells chic and well-made ladies fashions in Thai silk.

Palais Renaissance ❽ next door was built with the luxury goods market in mind, but it always seems to be deserted – further proof that Singapore's retailers cannot rely solely on the purchasing power of the city's well-heeled minority.

Seemingly unperturbed by the rampant consumerism in the vicinity, the dignified **Thai embassy** enjoys an idyllic spot within a fenced-off garden, a rare sight in downtown Orchard Road. But right beside it, past an alfresco café, it is business as usual in the shops of the **International Building** ❾ on Orchard Road. Orchard MRT station is just across the road.

Mural on Orchard Road

Shophouse facades

Route 3

Chinatown

This tour is an introduction to the Chinese side of Singapore – or rather what is left of the vitality of the city's Asian quarter now that all the furious restoration work is complete. Sadly, much of the colourful and noisy chaos generated by the enthusiastic salesmen and artisans has disappeared. Sewage no longer runs down the gutters at the roadside and damp and musty smells no longer emanate from inside the dilapidated shophouses.

The old Chinese quarter that Raffles established has spruced itself up and is now stealing the limelight from other parts of Singapore. But do not expect to find anything exotic – there are no opium dens and no unhygienic food stalls. What is on display in Singapore is really 'Chinatown for Beginners': immaculately restored streets with shophouses painted in pastel shades, tidy shops and appetising restaurants. But a walk through the maze of narrow alleys and past the lively market stalls will still provide a glimpse of the original Chinatown. Allow about six hours for the full tour.

Sri Mariamman Temple

There is an Indian temple in the heart of Chinatown. The ★★ **Sri Mariamman Temple** ⓐ with its smooth white exterior walls makes a strange starting point for this tour. It is situated on South Bridge Road between Pagoda Street and Temple Street and can be reached either by taxi or by a Singapore trolley. It is impossible to miss the brightly coloured pyramid of deities above the main entrance – a characteristic feature of Hindu temples. The pairs of shoes by the entrance give a clear message: visitors may only enter barefoot. This is the oldest Hindu temple in Singapore, and it is dedicated to the goddess Mariamman. It was built in 1827 by a wealthy merchant, initially out of wood but later restored with stone. It is the annual site of Thimiti, the fire-walking festival, a ritual dedicated to the goddes Droba-Devi, when the faithful work themselves into a trance and walk over burning embers to fulfil their vows.

Diagonally opposite the temple is a traditional chemist's shop, ★ **Eu Yan Sang** ④ (239 South Bridge Road; Mon–Sat 8.30am–6pm) supplies the Chinese with the exotic herbs that are said to cure every kind of minor ailment. Even if they have little faith in their own medicine, the Chinese furtively glance inside where they can read about ginseng and other herbal cures and inhale the aromatic perfumes. On sale here are birds' nests. To the Chinese, the birds' saliva that holds the nests together is a protein-rich delicacy.

Aspects of Chinatown

Follow South Bridge Road to the south and then turn left at the next corner into a small, gently climbing road called **Ann Siang Hill**. On the right-hand side stands a tastefully restored, three-storey building with gleaming, green roof tiles. When it rains, the water pours down and creates a kind of curtain around the house. This is no accident, as the Chinese believe that the rain curtain helps to 'keep money within'.

A few yards further on the left is **Club Street**, so-called because of the numerous club houses that the various di-

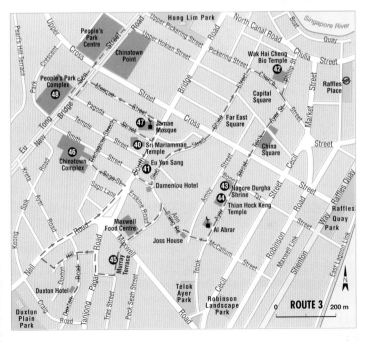

Chinese love bright colours

Inside Wak Hai Cheng Bio

alect groups set up here in the early part of the 19th century. These centres were important in helping to get new arrivals established. Only a few of these club houses, now known as 'associations', have survived. In their place behind renovated facades, traditional hotels such as the **Damenlou Hotel** (*see Accommodation, page 95*), have opened up. Nearly all the entrances have had to adopt the simple doors required by the Singaporean government as part of the facelift. Visually, they may be preferable, but they do not fit in with the Chinese love of bright colours and rich ornamentation.

Many homes had changed hands by the time restoration work was completed. The original owners either lacked the means to maintain the property or else they were unable to prove ownership, since, in the past, property had been handed down by word of mouth only. In many cases, the government acquired the crumbling buildings for a very small sum, safe in the knowledge that restored real estate in Chinatown could be leased out for huge sums.

With the horrendous rents that are now requested, more and more of the houses are being used by traders, advertising agencies, sound studios and the legal profession. In the evening when the offices close, the streets that once throbbed with life around the clock are now peaceful. At the end of Club Street, continue over Cross Street and straight along **China Street**, but take a wander down the narrow side lanes. All the old shophouses have been splendidly restored as this is a conservation district.

At the end of China Street, turn right into busy **Church Street**. Cross over at the nearest pedestrian lights and then turn left into narrow **Phillip Street**. On the corner stand the weathered walls of the ★★ **Wak Hai Cheng Bio Temple ⑫**, built in 1826 by the Teochew community shortly after their arrival in Singapore as a gesture of thanksgiving for their safe passage.

On **Telok Ayer Street**, on the left-hand side, is the huge **China Square** food court. Opposite, the entire street block bordered by Pekin and China streets is now **Far East Square**. A stroll through the restored shophouses occupied by retail outlets and restaurants, and the **Fuk Tak Chi Museum** (daily 10am–10pm) displaying over 200 artefacts from old Chinatown, provides a glimpse into the way of life of the early immigrants.

On the right by the corner of **Boon Tat Street** stands the **Nagore Durgha Shrine ⑬**. Its facade of columns and towers is an architectural compendium. Moslems from southern India worship at the shrine which is the burial site of Shahul Hamid Nagore, one of the great personalities in Moslem culture.

To the rear stands the richly decorated entrance to the ★★ **Thian Hock Keng Temple ⑭** (Temple of Heavenly

Thian Hock Keng

Happiness), the oldest and most interesting of all the temples in Singapore. A *joss house*, as the little altars were known, stood here as early as 1821. It had been built by immigrants from Fukien Province for Ma Chu Po, the 'patron saint' of mariners. At that time, the harbour was only a short distance away but, because so much land has since been reclaimed from the sea, it is now well inland. The present, spacious site dates from 1841, when the Chinese, who were prospering in Singapore, were able to afford tiles from Holland and wrought iron from Scotland. During renovations in 1999, a silk scroll bearing the handwriting of Qing Emperor Guang Xu (1871–1908) was discovered in the temple.

Thian Hock Keng

Only a few yards further on, but easily missed, stands the third sacred building on Telok Ayer Street: the modest **Al Abrar Mosque** which was built by Moslem Indians in 1855.

Enough of holy places. The sizzling food stands at the next junction are sure to turn the mind to more prosaic requirements. After a bite to eat and some welcome refreshments turn right into McCallum Street. A *joss house* at the end is open to the devout.

Local vegetable store

Make a short detour to the right into Amoy Street. Since its restoration, the smart premises have been snapped up by the business community. At the corner of Amoy Street and McCallum Street, a narrow, unnamed alley passes to the right of the *joss house* and a flight of steps leads up to **Ann Siang Road**.

Turn left towards a number of lavishly and lovingly restored houses. These show clearly that lessons have been learnt from the first unimaginative attempts at wholesale renovation. Continue along Kadayanallur Street, which soon joins the wide **Maxwell Road**. On the right-hand side is another **Food Centre**.

On the other side of Maxwell Road, the pedestrian-only ★ **Murray Terrace** ⑮ or Food Alley is devoted almost entirely to restaurants *(see Food and Drink pages 71–8).* A large board provides a key to each restaurant and the type of food it serves.

Cut through to **Tanjong Pagar Road** via **Cook Street**. The three-storey shophouses here were renovated some time ago and they now house attractive new shops with colourful shutters. Beware of the foot reflexology massage that is offered at No. 28a (and other places). Anyone not used to having the reflex zones on their feet massaged vigorously may find the process extremely painful.

A signpost indicates the route to ★ **Duxton Hill**, a fully restored quarter now home to Singapore's smart set. Take a stroll up and down Duxton Road, past all the beautiful shops, Western-style bars and the elegant **Duxton Hotel**.

Windows on the world

36

On the right-hand side, at a point on Duxton Hill where there are cobblestones between the houses and the decorative cultivated areas, a passageway cuts through to Neil Road (11am–9pm only). Look out for the wide glass door beneath '51 Neil Road'. This passage leads into a long complex of buildings to which 16 shophouses were linked. As well as several shops, there is also an interesting exhibition about the early 19th-century fishing village of **Tanjong Pagar**. Its Malay inhabitants were called *Orang Laut* or, roughly translated, 'the sea nomads'.

Enter Neil Road through the main gateway and then turn right. Many of the restored premises in the arcades are now either 'eating houses' – simple restaurants – or 'tea houses', e.g. **Yixing Xuan** (23 Neil Road, tel: 226 1646) with its large selection of teacups and teapots, and **Tea Chapter** (9A–11A Neil Road, tel: 226 1175). (*See Shopping, page 81.*)

The Chinese do not just drink tea, they celebrate it, whether at home or in the special tea houses that offer a wide variety of teas. Yellow tea is the most expensive, green tea the cheapest. The temperature of the water is the decisive factor. It should reach a temperature of 95°C/203°F, but not boiling point. Experts rely on their sense of hearing, laymen watch for a cherry-sized bubble to rise up from the base of the glass jug. Then the water is hot enough to warm up the tiny teapot, before it can be filled half full with tea leaves. The first infusion cleans the tea. Then the tea is left to brew for 30 seconds before the almost clear liquid is poured into slender, porcelain cups about the same size as a sherry glass. Do not start to drink yet, though. First take a sniff and absorb the aroma. The cup must be brought up to the mouth between thumb, forefinger and middle finger. A barbarian will drain his cup in one sip, but the Chinese take three. Now on to the next round. The tea leaves can be re-used up to five more times, but for each new brew, the water must infuse for an extra 10 minutes. Spicy 'tea eggs' are served as snacks. These are hard-boiled in tea-flavoured water.

Follow Neil Road northwards and into **South Bridge Road**, passing some tall, unsightly residential blocks. Until the 1960s, Sago Lane was where elderly, childless Chinese came to die, but the area has since been flattened to make way for new buildings.

Shops on the left in **Sago Street** sell traditional Chinese goods, e.g. Chinese healing oil from Fong Moon Kee at No. 16. The street was named after the numerous sago factories which used to operate here. On the left-hand side, steps lead up to the ★★ **Chinatown Complex** ⓭, a chaotic, but fascinating Chinese market. Stalls here sell not just clothes and household goods, but also, on the up-

A popular souvenir

per floor, typical Chinese fare, which is tasty, often spicy and very affordable – an experience worth savouring. Down in the basement an extraordinary range of ingredients is on sale – from live fish, reptiles and poultry to glorious fresh fruit, flowers and vegetables. The place is usually crowded well into the evening.

Since the renovation work in modern Chinatown was completed, many new tourist-orientated souvenir shops have opened. Formerly the various tradesmen such as tailors and basket-makers were clustered together in **Trengganu Street**, **Smith Street** and **Temple Street**. The once famed Cantonese opera house, Lai Chun Yuen, stands at the corner of Trengganu and Smith streets.

Turn left into **Pagoda Street** and then left again into South Bridge Road. Only a few yards further on stands the ★ **Jamae Mosque** ㊼, with its distinctive pagoda-like minarets. Moslems from southern India's Coromandel Coast have worshipped here since 1835. Turn down **Mosque Street** to reach the multi-storey shopping centres that are patronised by the local people. Two footbridges cross the busy New Bridge Road and Eu Tong Sen Street.

The ★★ **People's Park Complex** ㊽ on the left comprises several floors and has a bewilderingly colourful array of shops selling jewellery, leather goods, fabrics and hi-fis. But do not expect to find any special bargains here or at the **People's Park Centre** (nearest MRT station: Outram) nearby. Cheap and cheerful food stalls in the centre's basement stay busy for most of the day.

Shopaholics can cross from the northern end into **Chinatown Point** via a covered footbridge. The architects who worked on this project tried hard to create a stylish environment for shoppers. Chrome and glass predominate around spiral walkways lined with attractive shops. The goods on offer are unusual and of high quality, and are therefore not cheap.

Chinatown Point
Sago Street

Route 4

Little India

Visitors to Singapore who follow their noses will eventually find themselves in Little India – led there by the powerful aroma of curry and other exotic spices that seems to permeate the whole of this fascinating quarter. But Little India is also a feast for the eyes. Saris interwoven with gold thread, shimmering silk on display in the fabric stores

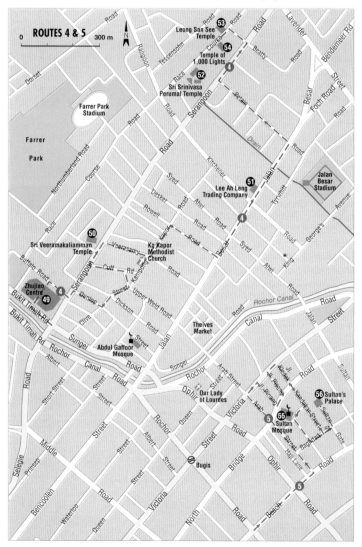

The Zhujiao Centre

and glittering gems and precious metals in the jewellery shops. The taste buds will also be in for a treat, as no food is more strongly spiced than that of southern India. Allow three hours to be swept away into the exotic world of the Indian subcontinent. Start in the morning because in the late afternoon there is a risk that the temples will be closed.

39

Little India is also the focus of Hindu festivals (*see pages 67–9*). Those lucky enough to be in Singapore during Deepavali, the Hindu New Year, will find Little India a riot of lights, lamps and garlands. Rather more macabre is Thaipusam, a two-day period of atonement when people may pierce skewers through their flesh.

Serangoon Road is the main artery in Little India. This tour begins in the south on the corner with Bukit Timah Road. The relatively modern ★★ **Zhujiao Centre** 🟡 is a multi-storey maze of colourful market stalls. The sight of goldsmiths selling their ornate earrings, necklaces and bracelets is reminiscent of a scene from *A Thousand and One Nights*. Prices vary from day to day as the price of gold fluctuates. A chart in every shop gives the price per gram of the worked gold.

Serangoon Road

A tour up, down and around the centre is like a voyage of discovery: there are fabric sellers, shoemakers, food stands and little stalls where garlands are made for visitors to the temple. And remember to pay a visit to the **Wet Market** in the basement. This section, which overflows with vegetables, fish and meat, gets its name from the hosepipes that, in line with Singaporean regulations, constantly spray the floor with water. And lingering as a backdrop to everything else is the pervasive aroma of the hot spices that are used to flavour Indian curries.

At the rear of the complex ★ **Buffalo Road** runs parallel to Bukit Timah Road. During the first 30 years of

Personalities of Little India

Sri Veeramakaliamman Temple Hindu images

the 20th century, *kerbau* (the Malay word for cattle) grazed here, but the Indian immigrants later turned the district into a trading quarter, specialising in buying and selling gold. However, the furious pace of Singaporean change has not spared Little India either. The favoured approach here was not so much to simply maintain the old buildings, but to renovate them in the old style – all financed by higher rents. As a result, most of the long-established jewellery shops moved into the Zhujiao Centre.

Follow Buffalo Road as far as Serangoon Road and then turn left. Trade keeps everyone busy on this lively thoroughfare. The windows of the shops where the Indian women buy the material for their saris are piled high with brightly coloured rolls of fabric. The same shops fit little girls with frilly pastel-coloured dresses and lace.

Turn right at the next corner into **Dunlop Street** where, under the **Little India Arcade**, there are tiny shops crammed to the ceiling with goods. Souvenir stalls abound in an open courtyard selling incense sticks, ayurvedic herbal oils and handicrafts from India. Unfortunately, these stores are gradually having to make way for sleek facades and spacious salesrooms.

Cut through Clive Street to get to Upper Weld Road. At the next junction turn sharp left into **Cuff Road**, where some smart Indian restaurants are situated. The tables at these restaurants are clean and neatly laid, and no one would dare to eat with their fingers. Few would object, however, if you ignored your cutlery in the basic but clean and cheap food halls of Serangoon Road. Turn right at the Cuff Road junction.

The ★ **Sri Veeramakaliamman Temple** ⑳ (daily 6.30am–noon, 5–9pm, Fri–Sat until 9.30pm) is on the left side of Serangoon Road. Few people will notice the plain external walls, although they may spot the colourful en-

Inside Sri Veeramakaliamman

trance tower; what attracts the Hindu faithful here is the ornate, black statue dedicated to Kali, Shiva's consort.

Colourful clothing

Diagonally opposite is **Veerasamy Road**. Even on Sunday, when the majority of shops are closed, the streets here in the heart of Little India are always alive. Groups of men stand around on street corners. Many of them will be just visiting friends and family as, during the week, they probably work away from home on building sites.

Ahead lies a longish walk. Follow **Kampung Kapor Road** (one of the side roads used to be a famous 'red light' area), **Rowell Road** and **Jalan Besar** as far as the **Lee Ah Leng Trading Company ⑤** (No. 267), a ramshackle bird centre. From inside their beautiful, hand-made bamboo or wire cages, the birds try to outdo each other with their singing. However, this is not a place for the animal rights activist.

Look out for the delightful old dwellings in Chinese baroque style along ★ **Petain Road**. Colourful tiles with flower decorations brighten up the green facades, making an attractive subject for photographers.

Return to Serangoon Road and cross over. Thanks to the generosity of a prosperous Indian entrepreneur, the ★ **Sri Srinivasa Perumal Temple ㊿** (daily 6.30am–noon, 5–9pm, Fri–Sat until 9.30pm) was fully restored in the 1960s and is popular as one of the start- and end-points of the annual Thaipusam Festival procession.

41

Where **Beatty Road** joins **Racecourse Road**, it is the Buddhist gods for a change who attract the crowds. The ★ **Leong San See Temple ㊾** is an impressive sight with golden dragons crouching on ochre roof tiles. The hubbub inside the temple contrasts with the silent reverence of Hindu temples. The large space at the back is dedicated to the dead. It is interesting to watch the relatives making offerings of food to their ancestors. In accordance with the notice, fish and meat may not be placed on the sacrificial table. The stench of food rotting in the sweltering heat would put even the most stoical Chinese off his prayers.

Leong San See Temple

On the other side of the road, the famous ★ **Temple of 1,000 Lights ㊿** (daily 7.30am–4.30pm), officially known as the Sakya Muni Buddha Gaya Temple, outshines all other Buddhist temples. Worshippers may illuminate the seated Buddha for a contribution of S$5. No one is allowed to touch the statue, but there is more to it than meets the eye. Beneath the Buddha is the entrance to a kind of grotto, in which the dying Buddha is portrayed. This temple represents the life's work of a Thai monk who died in 1976. Vutthisasara, as he was known, also provided the temple with a piece of bark – apparently from the tree where Buddha was sitting when he found enlightenment – and this precious relic is now worshipped.

Temple of 1,000 Lights

The best way to return to the city centre is by taxi.

Route 5

Arab Street

A place to meet the people

The district by the Rochor River was called Kampong Glam even at the time of the Sultan of Johor. It was to here that the Malayan ruler withdrew when he ceded Singapore to the British. The Malays that lived here then and the immigrants who arrived later from the Middle East, Pakistan, India and the Indonesian islands had one thing in common: they were all Moslems. That is why a purely Islamic quarter grew up very early on and it was named after the main street, Arab Street. The pavements are still the scenes of lively business activity, just like the bazaars, and the faithful are still called to prayer by the muezzins. Remember that haggling over prices is the norm in these parts too. This tour is less about seeing the sights, more about seeing the people: it is a glimpse into the lives of the Singaporean Moslems. During Ramadan, the streets remain quiet until sunset (*see Culture, page 67*). Allow a good three hours for this walk, but bargain-hunters will need to set aside more time. Doing deals in the Moslem quarter can take a long time.

Take the MRT Train to Bugis Street and then head southeast along Rochor Road as far as **Beach Road**. This used to be the coast road until the land reclamation project began. Here too, a whole series of narrow shophouses remain and as yet no restoration plans have been implemented. For many years, the merciless tropical climate has been taking its toll on the stone walls which are now beginning to crumble badly. Between roof tiles and in cracks in the wall, where it would seem nothing would grow, vegetation has taken root. And yet, despite the structural decay, commercial activity continues on the ground floor, while families live upstairs. Take a walk down the narrow alleys which branch off to the left and see the washing hanging out to dry from the windows. There is a smell of slightly burnt rice, aromatic herbs, of rubbish and mildew.

Arab Street – full to overflowing

★★ **Arab Street** really does do justice to the legendary enterprise of the Arabs. Traders selling basketware, leather goods and brass, batik materials and traditional Moslem clothing jostle beneath the shaded arcades. Many shops simply cannot cope with so many goods, but thankfully there is the 'five foot way', the five-foot wide corridor that fronts all shophouses, which can be stacked high with wares, regardless of whether there is room for the passers-by. It is easy to become entangled in a stand of leather bags or ensnared by a display of batik shawls. Have a good wander round and then order a tea in one of the cafés. The ma-

jority of other customers will probably be male. In accordance with tradition, most Islamic women who go out on to the streets cover their heads and some also wear a veil over their nose and mouth.

Now turn right twice, first into **Victoria Street** and then into the narrow **Jalan Pinang** alley from where the golden dome of the Sultan Mosque is visible, although it has to be approached from the other side. Turn left into **North Bridge Road**, another lively shopping street where it is not difficult to find unusual souvenirs.

Explore deeper into the strange world of the bazaar by making a short zigzag. Turn left into **Jalan Pisang**, right into **Victoria Street** and then right again into **Jalan Kledek**. Take a look in one of the simple restaurants and watch the *roti prata* show. A few acrobatic movements and the lumps of dough are transformed into wafer-thin pancakes. These are then baked on the hot plate and sprinkled with sugar or hot spices. Delicious!

Cross North Bridge Road and proceed a short way along **Kandahar Street**. Turn right into **Muscat Street** and ahead stands the **Sultan Mosque** ❸ (Fri 9–11.30am, 2.30–4pm, otherwise 9am–1pm, 2–4pm). The striking

Sultan Mosque

43

domed roof with its distinctive Arabic features forms part of the biggest mosque in Singapore. It is also the centre of the Islamic faith in the city. Filming and taking photographs is not allowed. Women visitors who do not completely cover their arms and legs will be given a long cloak at the entrance. While the men kneel on the carpeted floor to pray, the women must stay in the gallery.

Leave the mosque district via ★ **Bussorah Mall**, once a dilapidated lane, but now a smart, traffic-calmed avenue with palm trees and attractively restored houses. This is the historic heart of the old Kampong Glam district and, in 1989, parts of it were classified as a conservation area.

The fine two-storey shophouses in **Baghdad Street** (Nos. 2–10) stand on a very small surface area. Looking rather neglected, in an untidy cul-de-sac called **Sultan Gate**, stands the **Sultan's Palace** ❺, a building of historical significance. Built as royal residence for Sultan Hussein of Johor in 1867, it was occupied by his descendants until 1999, when they were resettled and compensated so that the palace could be preserved as the Malay Heritage Centre.

Delicate blends at Jamal Kazura

Return to North Bridge Street via Baghdad and Kandahar streets. Turn left and sniff the air for the delicate blends of perfume at **Jamal Kazura Aromatics** (No. 728). At the junction of North Bridge Road and Arab Street, a difficult choice lies in store: selecting one of the numerous, excellent Moslem restaurants with their strongly-spiced, but always pork-free dishes.

You may take a taxi or walk to the Bugis MRT station.

Sentosa Ferry Terminal

Route 6

Sentosa, Singapore's playground

Only 250m (275 yds) or so from Singapore's main island, the emphasis is on leisure and fun. Sentosa Island
used to be a burial place for victims of the local pirates
(when it was called Blakang Mati – Back of the Dead) and
then served as a fortress for the British.

However, in the 1970s the Singaporean government re-
named the island and unashamedly transformed it into a
pleasure park. Nothing is left to chance here. The organisation and infrastructure on the island are magnificent.
As masses of visitors arrive every weekend, careful crowd
management is required. If possible avoid the weekend,
but do allow a full day and remember to take a swimming costume. All the main attractions can be reached
on buses or via the monorail. The following route has been
planned in such a way that the highlights may all be vis-
ited without backtracking.

*A dragon greets cable car
visitors to Sentosa*

The ★ **World Trade Centre** at the water's edge on the
main island is the starting point for this route (*see page
88*). As well as some attractive shops and restaurants, it
has world-class moving exhibitions such as the Guinness
World of Records Exhibition and the world-renowned
Madame Tussaud Wax Works. The **Maritime Showcase**
(Tues–Fri 10.30am–6.30pm, Saturday and Sunday
10.30am–8.30pm) contains a model of the harbour.

The first attractions on Sentosa can easily be reached
on foot from the **Ferry Terminal**. Turn to the left and
follow the directions on the board to the **Sentosa Food
Centre** ❺❼. Here, over a dozen spotlessly clean hawker
stalls provide practically every available cuisine in Sin-

gapore. This is the ideal place for a second breakfast or an early lunch.

★★ **Fantasy Island** (daily 10am–6pm), directly behind the food centre, is probably the biggest draw on Sentosa. It is a gigantic waterpark with something for everyone, young or old. The flumes, white-water rapids, eight-track slide and other watery entertainments are surrounded by walls modelled on an ancient Maya settlement. The admission system is rather unusual: when the entrance charge is paid, a likeness of the payee is recorded on computer as proof of identity. Bathers may then circulate within the complex without cash and buy food and drink at the snack bar. All expenditure is totalled up and the account settled upon departure.

Fantasy Island

A white-knuckle experience of a different kind is on offer in ★ **Cinemania** (daily 11am–8pm), just to the right of Fantasy Island. Sit down, get strapped in and enjoy a rollercoaster ride or a journey through an abandoned gold mine, all from a seat in the cinema. Not for those of a feeble disposition.

Orchid Gardens is for the gardener and amateur botanist, who will be interested in the countless varieties of orchids arranged around a pond and the unusual 'Yin-shi' boulders.

45

The ★ **Fountain Gardens** , which extend as far as the ferry terminal, are not quite as colourful. Laid out in

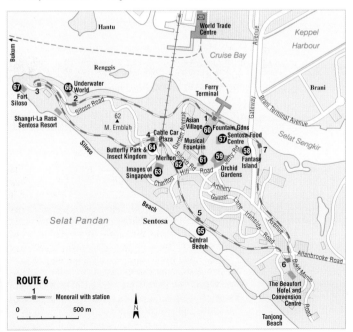

ROUTE 6

Monorail with station

0   500 m

N

Musical Fountain

Images of Singapore's history

a symmetrical pattern with fountains and over 100 different plant species, they are modelled on the gardens of European stately homes.

The glorious **Musical Fountain** comes to life every evening. This fabulous water- and light- show is accompanied by classical music played through loudspeakers (daily at half-hourly intervals from 5pm with night performances at 7.30pm, 8.30pm and 9.30pm including spectacular light and laser effects). You may want to come back to the fountain at the end of your tour of Sentosa as the ferry terminal is only a few minutes' walk away. Watching the water dance to music is a perfect conclusion to a day on Sentosa.

Children will probably prefer **Volcano Land 61** (daily 10am–7pm). This attraction features an ingenious rendering of a volcanic eruption in the labyrinth of a man-made mountain. The 35-m (115-ft) high **Merlion 62** (daily 9am–10pm) offers good panoramic views.

Next, make the climb up the hillside to the informative and extremely interesting history lesson in the exhibition halls of the ★★ **Images of Singapore 63** (daily 9am–9pm). Inside, life-sized figures tell the story of Singapore's early history, the wars, the road to independence and the harmony in which the different ethnic groups live. Nowhere else is the history of Singapore presented in such an entertaining way.

In the Pioneers exhibition you will see the conditions in which Chinese coolies were obliged to live – sometimes sharing with Indian convicts – and Henry Ridley and his rubber tree. You will also see Miss Joaquim and her orchid that became Singapore's national flower.

The Surrender Chambers show the ebb and flow of events seen by Singapore in World War II. The British surrender to the Japanese; the Japanese occupy Singapore; the Japanese surrender to the Allies. The exhibition reveals how the more fortunate Singaporeans survived Japan's racial-purity purge.

Now take a stroll through the **Butterfly Park & Insect Kingdom Museum 64** (daily 9am–6.30pm), where more than 2,500 brightly coloured butterflies flit freely from flower to flower in a large enclosed garden. There is also a collection of preserved insects – over 4,000 – that includes the world's largest and rarest species.

Cable cars (daily 8.30am–9pm) leave from **Cable Car Plaza** to Mount Faber (on the main island) and back. The ★★ **trip** is well worth taking and affords some spectacular views of rusty freighters, gleaming white liners and the busiest container port in the world. Unfortunately, unless a lens filter is fitted, the reflecting cable car windows will spoil any photographs.

Climb out of the cable car, jump on to the monorail

and travel from Station 4 to Station 5 (Beruk Station) and **Central Beach 65**. This lagoon with its man-made beach of reddish sand is very popular with bathers, despite all the shipping traffic just offshore. Tents may be hired at Sentosa's only camp-site which is situated close by. The extensive New Siloso Beach is also worth a visit.

Further on, Monorail Station 6 is within walking distance of the Youth Hostel and also **The Beaufort Hotel & Convention Centre**, a luxurious hotel a little higher up. It has the biggest hotel swimming pool in Singapore and non-residents are welcome to stop off for a poolside drink.

Station 2 on the monorail is the starting point for the **Nature Walk/ Dragon Trail** through shady jungle vegetation and ★ **Underwater World 66** (daily 9am–9pm), Asia's biggest aquarium where countless tropical fish are kept in a huge tank. What makes Underwater World even more special, however, is the 100-m (110-yd) acrylic tunnel through the middle. Stand on the conveyor belt and watch the fish swimming around.

By the sea, but a longish walk away, the **Shangri-La Rasa Sentosa Resort** is another luxury hotel with recreational facilities and a crèche for younger guests.

In the underground passages of the old **Fort Siloso 67** (Station 3; daily 9am–7pm), exhibits and displays retell the ironic story of the battle for Singapore during World War II. The British were convinced Siloso's big guns would protect Singapore. Unfortunately, the guns pointed out to sea and the Japanese came through the jungle on bicycles with flat tyres. In the following siege, the British surrendered a few days before the Japanese planned to withdraw because of lack of supplies.

Take the monorail back to the ferry terminal, perhaps stopping at the **Asian Village** (10am–9pm) on the way to sample some food and watch a performance by one of the various cultural troupes.

Underwater World

Siloso Beach

Fort Siloso

Route 7

Jurong

The drained marshland to the west of Singapore has turned into one of the most important industrial locations on the island. Proximity to the container port was one factor in its development, but the existence of a good road network and the underground railway also played a part. 'Industrial parks' have been added and the flowerbeds and green spaces give some justification to this name. Between the docks and the city centre, spacious parkland provides rest and relaxation and, at the weekend, many city dwellers are attracted by the wildlife parks. The sights described here are not all within easy reach of each other and so do not easily lend themselves to a self-contained tour. The best way to get from one to the other is via the excellent public transport network, but it's not possible to cover them all in one day.

Chinese Garden

Not surprisingly, the ★ **Chinese Garden** ➏➑ on Yuan Ching Road (Mon–Sat 9am–7pm, Sun and public holidays 8.30am–7pm: nearest MRT station: Chinese Garden) is a favourite spot for happy couples to pose for their wedding photographs. Colourful pavilions and towers, delightful arched bridges and ponds dotted with sea roses and water lilies all make an idyllic backdrop. Everything is set in a meticulously tended 13-hectare (32-acre) Song-style garden, surrounded by the waters of the Jurong Lake. It is the perfect place to take a leisurely stroll, or to inhale the aromatic scents of the herb garden.

Japanese Garden

Next to the Chinese garden and accessible via a bridge, is the **Japanese Garden** ➏➒, also within the Jurong Lake (daily 9am–7pm). About the same size as its Chinese counterpart, the garden displays the main features of Japanese landscaping, such as a concern for detail, clear lines and simple forms. Although the shrubs in the stone garden, alongside the running water and waterfalls, have been positioned with considerable care, the impression is one of random planting. To appreciate the gardens fully, allow about 2½ hours for each.

The ★ **Singapore Science Centre/Omni Theatre** ➐➊ on Science Centre Road (Tues–Sun, 10am–6pm; nearest MRT station: Jurong East, then on foot or by bus No. 335) will enthrall children and technophiles for hours. All the secrets of science and technology are revealed. In a special 'hands-on' gallery, activities include a simulated flight landing. In the **Omni Theatre** a series of films is shown on a huge, hemispheric screen. Planetarium shows take place every hour 10am–9pm

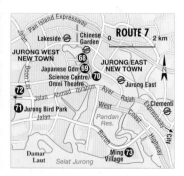

ROUTE 7 2 km

(except 1pm and 5pm). There is easily enough at the complex to keep visitors occupied for two hours.

★★ **Jurong Bird Park** ❼ on Jalan Ahmad Ibrahim (Mon–Fri 9am–6pm; Sat, Sun and public holidays 8am–6pm; nearest MRT station: Boon Lay, then bus Nos 194/251) has over 8,000 birds and 600 different species. Around 1,200 birds fly around in the biggest walk-in aviary in the world. Some 20 hectares (50 acres) of land are enclosed by a huge net. If **Breakfast with the Birds** (daily 9–11am) is too early, then watch one of the shows, such as the **JBP All Star Birdshow** when the flamingos dance to a Caribbean rhythm (daily 11am and 3pm). Another favourite with the crowds is the **Kings of the Skies Show** (daily 4pm) when eagles and falcons demonstrate their skills. The **Humming Bird Aviary** is yet another hot favourite. To make the most of the Bird Park, allow yourself a good 3 hours.

The electric chair exhibit at the Discovery Centre

49

The **Singapore Discovery Centre** ❼ out to the west on Upper Jurong Road (Tues–Fri 9am–7pm; Sat, Sun and public holidays 9am–8pm; nearest MRT station: Boon Lay, then by bus Nos 192/193) is a high-tech interactive centre devoted to Singapore's history and technological endeavours. Main attractions are a 9-m (30-ft) wide map containing 2,574 photographs of Singaporeans from all walks of life, the iWerks Theatre, which has a 5-storey high screen, a shooting gallery, motion simulator and many interactive games.

Magnificent Chinese porcelain in Ming dynasty-style is produced and sold at the ★★ **Ming Village** ❼ at 32 Pandan Road (daily 9am–5.30pm; nearest MRT station: Clementi, then bus No. 78). Visitors can see freshly thrown clay turn into an elegant, classical-style, hand-painted object of beauty. A metre-high (3-ft) vase with the characteristic blue motifs costs in the region of S$8,000. The staff will be happy to wrap and despatch home any fragile items. To send a large vase will cost about S$330.

Flamingoes at Jurong Bird Park

Exhibit at the Malay Village

Shade of colour

Route 8

The Malay Geylang Serai quarter to the Peranakan Katong quarter

The Malays have clearly stayed in control in Geylang Serai. On the streets, the women and girls wear colourful dress and cover their hair with Islamic-style cloths or hoods. Many of the men wrap the traditional *sarungs* around their hips. In the lively Malay markets the national traditions are still very much in evidence. Appetising aromas waft from the many small snack bars and simple restaurants and it is hard to resist sampling some of the delicious Malay specialities.

There are treats for the taste buds too in the Katong quarter where clear traces of the Peranakans (*see page 9*) remain. The somewhat primitive shopping streets are lined by splendid old buildings. Nearby, wealthy Singaporeans live in detached houses, while the middle classes occupy rather plain residential blocks.

This tour involves a lot of walking, but to compensate there will be plenty of opportunities for breaks. Allow about four hours, preferably in the morning, when the streets are at their busiest.

The ideal starting point in Geylang Serai is the **Paya Lebar** MRT station. The ★★ **Malay Village** ❼ (daily 10am–10pm) is only a short distance away. The aim of this complex is to illustrate the history, culture and lifestyle of the Malays. Souvenir shops and restaurants serving Malay specialities have taken over the traditional wooden houses with their pointed gables.

Displays in a small **Cultural Museum** shed light on the Malay heritage. The basic wooden huts in the **Kampong Nostalgia** take visitors back to the Geylang Serai of the

1950s and a magnificent wedding celebration is enacted with the aid of puppets. Romantics will not want to miss **Lagenda Fantasi** (daily between noon and 9pm as required). Ali Baba and other oriental legends are enchantingly retold using multivision effects.

On the other side of Geylang Serai lies the ★★ **Geylang Serai Market**  (daily, early in the morning until dusk, during Ramadan until late into the night). *Serai* is the Malay word for lemongrass, a spice that used to be cultivated here and continues to be an important ingredient in Malay cooking.

Geylang Serai Market

Also gone forever are the many little mills that converted the grass to citronella cooking oil. The market is a maze of tightly packed stalls, many of which sag under the weight of fabrics, household goods, jewellery and artificial flowers. In the adjoining food market, various aromas waft through the air, enticing shoppers into snack bars. Despite the crowds, nobody pushes or shoves as the shoppers shuffle past the mountains of goods.

Return to Geylang Serai and cross Changi Road. On the left-hand side, the busy **Joo Chiat Complex** ⑦ shopping centre sells a wide range of typically Malay goods, but it is not as interesting as the Geylang Serai market.

51

Many businesses along **Joo Chiat Road** are run from the ground floor of stone shophouses, which have long outlasted the old Malay structures made from wood. Many

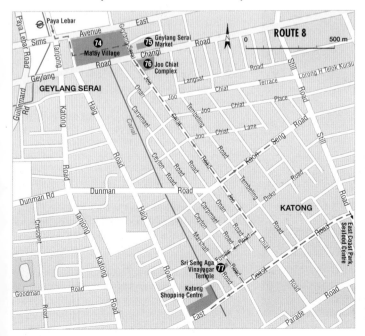

traditional professions survive here in the same way as the Chinese cottage industries (*see page 15*). At **Kway Guan Huat** (No. 95) crêpe mixture for spring rolls is still made by hand in the morning and then sold throughout the day. A workshop diagonally opposite produces hand-made rattan furniture, which is then displayed on the pavement.

About 700m (750yds) further on, make a brief detour to the left into ★ **Koon Seng Road** to discover the grand Peranakan houses. Their facades, richly decorated with colourful tiles, testify to the wealth of the original owners. They also indicate that this is the right route to **Katong**. Take a close look at the shape of the air-vents above the windows. What look like butterflies are, in fact, bats. Like the Chinese, the Peranakans believed that these creatures brought good luck.

Sri Seng Aga Vinayagar Temple

Katong Bakery & Confectionery

One or two nightclubs are situated further along Joo Chiat Road. These do not open until much later when an unambiguous red light glows. There is, however, room for a place of worship: the **Sri Seng Aga Vinayagar Temple ⑰**. This fine-looking neighbourhood temple was built for the district's small Hindu community. The faithful come here to revere the elephant-headed god of wisdom, Ganesh, whose statue stands above the entrance.

At the end of the road, turn left into **East Coast Road**. The ★ **Katong Bakery & Confectionery** at No. 75 (daily 8am–7pm) sells delicious curry puffs and curry cakes, prepared to a traditional Peranakan recipe. For an air-conditioned environment, if the temperature rises, turn right along East Coast Road and make for the **Katong Shopping Centre**. Attractions here include the chance to sample birds' nests (*see Food and Drink, page 72*). Otherwise, head east on the left side of East Coast Road. Some basic *Nonya* restaurants serve *laksa* (rice noodles with fish in a spicy coconut milk sauce).

One interesting gallery is the **Katong Antique House** (No. 208). The owner, Peter Wee, is a descendant of an old Peranakan family and he will be happy to show you his collection of Peranakan antiques. Call 345 8544 to make an appointment. Also of interest are the pawnbrokers shops. Anything that is not redeemed within six months is put on sale. Occasionally, good jewellery and watches are sold at very reasonable prices. Do not pass the ★ **Daun Pandan Rice Dumpling** (No. 226) without trying either a delicious vegetarian dish or chunks of meat cooked in pandanus leaves.

Either end the tour here – or take a taxi and cool off by the ★ **East Coast Park**. During the day, walkers can enjoy miles of paths and cooling sea breezes, while fitness fanatics can choose between a number of different sporting facilities. In the evening, it is the food served in the numerous seafood restaurants that draws the visitors.

Seafood draws the visitors

Route 9

The other islands

There are about 52 islands off Singapore's 'mainland'. Few are accessible to tourists and only about half of them are inhabited. Malay fishermen and farmers living in rather primitive villages make up the majority of the population. However, it is on these *pulau*, the Malay word for island, that the other side of Singapore can still be seen.

Unfortunately, tourism is gaining ground on the more attractive islands and luxury hotels, beaches and leisure facilities will, the authorities hope, attract increasing numbers of visitors. A couple of islands are served by regular ferries. The only way to reach the others is to join a tour or hire a boat.

According to legend, ★ **Kusu Island** (Pulau Tembakul) is a giant turtle that became an island to save a Malay and a Chinese sailor from drowning. As a token of their gratitude, the Malaysian built a holy shrine and the Chinese built a temple.

Kusu Island does have two holy sites that support this tale: Malay pilgrims regularly make the trip to the **Keramat Abdul Rahman**, while, in the ninth month of the Chinese lunar calendar, the **Tua Pekong Temple** is the destination for a spectacular pilgrimage by boat. However, this attractive temple that stands above the water on stilts is worth a visit at any time of the year. Furthermore, there is a fine bathing beach within easy reach.

Kusu Island is 7km (4 miles) from Singapore's main island and no overnight accommodation is available. Boats leave from the World Trade Centre (Mon–Sat 10am and 1.30pm. The last return ferry is at 3.30pm. Additional ferries on Sun between 9am and 7.20pm, and the last return ferry is at 8pm).

St John's Island (Pulau Sakijang Bendera) is where Raffles anchored before meeting the Temenggong on the Singapore River in 1819. Although it was developed as a holiday resort in the 1970s, the island now attracts fewer visitors as one-third of it has been turned into a Marine Aquaculture Centre and another third into a detention centre for illegal immigrants. Plans to develop **Lazarus Island** into a tropical beach resort have been shelved and the island is now out of bounds.

Pulau Hantu (southwest of Sentosa) and **Sisters Islands** southwest of St John's) are favourite haunts of experienced divers who want to explore the clear waters and observe the abundant fish. Beware of the powerful currents off Pulau Hantu. No regular boat service exists, so

53

Family dip

the beaches and picnic sites here are usually empty. No overnight accommodation is available either and the only way to get to the island is to hire a boat by Clifford Pier or the World Trade Centre.

About 70 Malay families still live on the island of **Pulau Seking**. In their homes in the *kampung*, the traditional wooden houses still sit on stilts over the water; it is as if time has stood still. While many of the younger generation have left to work in the refineries or in the factories by the harbour, the old folk continue to fish, as they always have, in their *jongs* – hand-carved, long, narrow outriggers with bright canvas sails. To walk around the island will take about 30 minutes. Getting to the 4-sq km (1½-sq mile) rocky outcrop will take about 40 minutes (boats leave from Clifford Pier). The government has plans to 'develop' the island in the near future.

★ **Pulau Ubin** lies in the narrow Johor Strait between Malaysia and Singapore. Malay village life continues amid the luxuriant tropical vegetation, but the population is dwindling rapidly. Some 3,000 people once lived on the island, but now only about 400 remain in the simple wooden dwellings.

A 15-minute boat ride from the jetty in **Changi Village** is all it takes to reach Ubin. Ferries operate between 7am and 9pm, but only when 12 passengers are waiting. The island, which is twice as big as Sentosa, is popular with nature lovers who bring their tents and provisions in order to observe the wide variety of wildlife. While there, check out the **Ubin Lagoon Resort**, the ultimate adventure experience in Singapore. Officially opened in April 2000, it features three 'nested' swimming pools under a grove of trees, a 3-m (3-yd) high children's flying fox ride, open-air spas and an archery range. It is the first resort in Singapore to bring in all-terrain vehicles (ATVs) and create a challenging 500-m (547-yd) course for them.

Visitors wishing to explore the island on the unmade tracks should allow a full day. Mountain bikes, plus a simple map of the island, can be hired in the village (Yen Fa Bicycle Rental, daily 8am–5pm, S$3 per day). Taxis are also available (about S$20 per hour), but the drivers do not speak English. The best way to overcome this problem is to buy a map of the island at the cycle hire centre and then show the taxi driver the two sights that are essential viewing: the colourful **Thai Temple**, which was built by Thai monks, and the **Ma Chor Temple**, a magnificent Chinese structure by the seashore, from where Singapore's impressive skyline is visible.

Limestone is quarried in certain parts of the island and 'Blasting Areas' are indicated.

Pulau Ubin from Changi beach

Old quarry on Ubin

Further Sights

Alkaff Mansion

There are not that many tourist sights away from the main routes already described. Most of them can be reached easily as public transport is good. If necessary, take a taxi. On weekends and holidays, Singapore families head out of town to the gardens, leisure parks and the zoo, so, if possible, try to choose a weekday.

55

★ **Chettiar's Hindu Temple** at 15 Tank Road, west of Fort Canning Hill (daily 8am–noon and 5.30pm–8.30pm; nearest MRT station: Dhoby Ghaut, then on foot via Clemenceau Avenue, *see map on page 21*) is the popular name for the splendid **Sri Thandayuthapani Temple**, which was rebuilt in 1983 with funds from the wealthy Chettiar community of money lenders. One particularly impressive feature is the roof which is fitted with 48 windows that catch the rays of the rising and the setting sun. Crowds of devout Hindus fill the temple during the Hindu festivals, notably Thaipusam (*see page 67*).

The ★ **Alkaff Mansion** at 10 Telok Blangah Green on Mount Faber (best reached by taxi) was built in the 1920s by a wealthy Arab family by the name of Alkaff. Sumptuous gatherings were held at this magnificent mansion with its superb view of the coast and Sentosa Island. Lavish restoration work during the 1990s returned the splendour to the thick stone walls without destroying the nostalgic atmosphere. Guests at this opulent restaurant can choose from the **Mansion Hall** (Oriental/Western cuisine), the **Dining Room** (*rijstaffel*) and the **West Terrace** (for private functions only), but the speciality is definitely the colonial Dutch-Indonesian *rijstaffel*. Before dinner, enjoy a drink and watch the sun set in the **Verandah Bar**. Table reservations are recommended.

The mansion's dining room

Haw Par Villa

★★ Haw Par Villa Tiger Balm Gardens at 262 Pasir Panjang Road (daily 9am–6pm; nearest MRT station: Clementi [W8], then SBS bus No. 10) is a beautifully landscaped Chinese mythological theme park. Every conceivable god, hero, beauty, demon and beast from the world of myth and legend is assembled here – much to the delight of the locals. One of the main attractions is the grotesque recreation of Chinese mythical hell called the **Ten Courts of Hell**. The exhibits depict all manner of fiendish torture in the nether world, some of which are quite stomach-turning: evil-doers being disembowelled and boiled in hot oil, impaled on spikes or sliced in two are just a few of the more graphic scenes.

Originally the home of the well-known Aw family, the villa was funded by the two 'Tiger Balm' brothers, Aw Boon Haw and Aw Boon Par, who made their fortune from Tiger Balm, the aromatic ointment that is used the world over to treat headaches and minor ailments.

Botanic Gardens

The **★ Botanic Gardens** (daily 5am–midnight) is a huge, green oasis in the middle of the city, not far from Orchard Road. Opened in 1859, the site has recently been enlarged to 52 hectares (128 acres), and other changes include improvements to the infrastructure, guided walks and, at the entrance in Cluny Road, a modern visitor centre with audio-visual aids. The existing areas, such as the orchid gardens and herb and spices beds, have also been smartened up. Home to more than 2,500 plants, including Singapore's national flower *Vanda Miss Joaquim*, this delightful park attracts many picnickers and strollers.

The **★ Bukit Timah Nature Reserve** (nearest MRT station: Newton [N4], then bus No. 67, 170 or 171 or TIBS bus No. 182) is, for the most part, unspoilt jungle at the heart of the island, just 12km (7 miles) from the city centre. Visitors can explore this wildlife reserve on well-marked footpaths and a brochure showing the possible circular tours is available at the entrance. At 162.5m (534ft), **Bukit Timah Hill** is the highest point on the island and it is worth making the climb to view Seletar reservoir. Allow a few hours, even half a day, to do justice to this fascinating reserve, but do not forget to apply plenty of mosquito repellent. While the pestilential insects have been driven out of the city, walkers will be mercilessly attacked unless they are well protected. The visitor centre is on Hindhede Drive, tel: 468 5736.

The ★★ **Zoological Garden** on Mandai Lake Road (daily 8.30am–6pm; nearest MRT station: Ang Mo Kio [N9], then SBS bus No. 138, or Choa Chu Kang Station [N21], then TIBS bus No. 927) houses over 2,000 animals. Most of them are kept, not in cages or behind wire, but in spacious, humane enclosures surrounded by ditches. Sometimes called the 'open zoo', it is noted for its work in breeding orang-utans – visitors are, therefore, cordially invited to 'Breakfast or High Tea with the Orang-Utan' (daily 9am or 4pm). After breakfast, the next highlight of the day is a photograph with the apes and a glass of orange juice. The 30-minute Animal Shows in the amphitheatre are also worth watching (daily 10.30am, 11.30am, 2.30pm, 3.30pm), while the Polar Bear Show takes place every day at 10.05am, 1.05pm and 4.45pm. Elephant and camel rides are also available. Without making any longer stops, a full tour of the zoo can be completed in about 45 minutes on the shuttle bus. But why hurry?

The ★★ **Night Safari Park** on Mandai Lake Road near the zoo (daily 7.30pm–midnight; nearest MRT stations as for Zoological Garden above) is open at night so that animal lovers can observe nocturnal animals in their natural state. Altogether, 1,200 animals are kept in 47 different habitats within the park. A 45-minute tour by train passes seemingly open and discreetly lit enclosures. Flash photography is forbidden. There are also three walking tours that together take about two hours (2.8km/1¾ miles). No one need be worried about going astray in the dark or treading on a lion's tail. Staff posted at regular intervals make sure everyone is on the right route. Evening meals are available in the adjoining restaurant either from an *à la carte* menu or a very reasonably priced buffet. To see the animals at their most active, try to get round the park before 9.30pm; the last tour starts at 11.15pm.

The ★ **Mandai Orchid Gardens** are a 15-minute walk from the zoo on Mandai Lake Road (daily 8.30am–5.30pm; nearest MRT stations: Ang Mo Kio [N9], then SBS bus No. 138, or Choa Chu Kang station [N21], then TIBS

Jungle warriors, Bukit Timah

Feeding time

Mandai miracles

bus No. 927). The many species of orchids growing here are cultivated in a mixture of charcoal and brick; some clamber up poles in banks of vivid profusion, while others hang in delicate sprays from suspended pots. This 4-hectare (10-acre) garden has one of the world's finest orchid displays.

Lovers of these beautiful plants are able to enjoy the colourful blooms in the gardens throughout the whole year – and, if they wish, take them home. The 'Orchid Gift Box Service' will deliver the elegant flowers to any address in the world.

Birds are greatly admired by the Chinese and they are a common sight in many Singaporean flats. Owners frequently spend hours teaching their beloved pets to sing, sometimes with the aid of cassettes – a well-trained bird can be worth several thousand dollars.

58

Birds at Seng Poh

Bird lovers congregate with their birds every Sunday morning at about 10am in the **Seng Poh Coffee Shop** (corner of Tiong Bahru and Seng Poh Road; nearest MRT station: Tiong Bahru). Undisturbed by the traffic noise, the birds give of their best. The cages are not placed close together by accident or through lack of space – this is how beginners learn from their more advanced friends. Visitors to the café are, of course, able to enjoy the avian concert over a cup of coffee.

★★ **Singapore Harbour** is used by 400 shipping lines. At any one time, there are over 800 ships and 100,000 containers in port. It handles some 850 million tonnes of cargo every year. There are two ways tourists can view the vast harbour area – from the water or the air.

A boat trip around the harbour takes tourists past tiny offshore islands and many more or less seaworthy vessels

Singapore's Clifford Pier

that lie at anchor further out to sea. The cost of a lunch or an evening meal is included in the price.

Perhaps the most romantic way is to make the trip in a Chinese junk, such as the *Fairwind* (from Clifford Pier, Eastwind Organisation, tel: 533 3432; daily at 10.30am, 3pm and 6pm).

The three-hour 'Port Discovery Tour' run by Sentosa Discovery Tours (tel: 277 9633; daily bookings with a minimum of five passengers) takes tourists behind the scenes in the computer-operated port.

If you get seasick, perhaps you should take to the air over the harbour on the cable car that links Mount Faber with Sentosa island via the World Trade Centre on the harbour edge (*see pages 46 and 88*).

Changi is the name of the ultra-modern airport and the nearby plain, prefabricated village. The coastal strip around the landing stage for the ferry to Pulau Ubin (*see Route 9, page 54*) and the marina where wealthy Singaporeans moor their boats are much more attractive areas. The beach is lovely for a leisurely stroll.

Changi is also the site of Singapore's biggest prison and **Changi Prison Chapel and Museum**, a memorial to the prisoner-of-war camp run by the Japanese during World War II (Mon–Sat 9.30am–4.30pm; nearest MRT station: Tanah Merah [E9], then SBS bus No. 2). Its focal point is the replica of a small wooden chapel hand-built by the allied soldiers as a symbol of hope. Photographs, documents and everyday objects exhibited in the nearby museum give some impression of the cruelty that the prisoners had to endure. James Clavell's famous novel *King Rat* (1962) powerfully describes the suffering of the prisoners-of-war in Changi.

The Chapel at Changi

Mangrove swamp takes up almost a third of the 17-hectare (42-acre) **Pasir Ris Park** on the northeast coast of Singapore (Pasir Ris Road; nearest MRT station: Pasir Ris [E12], then SBS bus No. 21 or 350). The birds and the marshy primeval forest that once covered a large part of Singapore can be seen from wooden decking. Pasir Ris is also Singapore's showpiece residential quarter.

Do not miss the ★ **Lian Shan Shuang Lin Monastery** at 184 E Jalan Toa Payoh (daily 9am–5pm; nearest MRT station: Toa Payoh – N6). Built in 1908, this impressive temple complex with its sweeping, green-tiled roofs, is situated amid new development by the expressway. Everywhere between the bright red walls, incense sticks and oil lamps burn in honour of Buddha. It is one of the biggest and, in the afternoon, one of the liveliest temples in all of Singapore.

Lian Shan Shuang Lin Monastery

Excursions

Malaysia and Indonesia are very close to Singapore so it is easy to make the short crossing, with organised tours or independently. To enter either country you need a passport valid for another six months. Malaysia allows you to stay two months without a visa, Indonesia three months. Anti-malaria tablets are recommended. The destinations below are for travellers with limited time: for all excursions, you can be back in Singapore within two days.

Causeway to Johor Bahru
Abu Bakar Mosque

Johor Bahru

This Malaysian town lies on the other side of the Causeway, about half an hour's drive away from the centre of Singapore. Fuel tanks have to be at least three-quarters full when vehicles leave Singapore, and the authorities check gauges to stop locals driving into Malaysia to buy cheap fuel. In Johor Bahru it soon becomes apparent that practically everything is cheaper in Malaysia, particularly textiles and arts and crafts.

Look for the **Istana Besar** (Sultan's Palace) in its beautiful garden, the **Abu Bakar Mosque** above the town and the **cemetery** which contains the splendid tombs of Johor's royal family.

Most Singapore taxis are not licensed for Malaysia, but plenty of buses journey between Singapore and Johor Bahru (express bus from Ban San Street/Rochor Canal Road or the slower SBS No. 170 from Queen Street). Organised bus tours take about three and a half hours. RMG Travel, tel: 220 1661. Buses leave at 9.30am every day.

Desaru

The 20-km (12-mile) sandy beach on the southeast coast of Malaysia is a favourite haunt for Singapore's well-to-do. There is always plenty going on in the hotels at weekends and during the holidays. A hire car is the ideal way of getting there, but organised bus tours are available. These take two days and the fare includes overnight accommodation. Siakson Coach Tours, tel: 336 0288. Buses leave at 9am every day.

Melaka

Melaka, on Malaysia's west coast almost 220km (135 miles) from Singapore, is a town with a long history. Until the 16th century, the town was ruled by a powerful sultan and his family, but they were deposed by the Portuguese. The Dutch arrived next, followed by the British.

Several buildings reflect a European influence. The **Stadthuys**, for example, was built in the mid-17th century by the Dutch. It now houses the **Historical Museum**, which documents the town's colonial heritage. In 1741, the Dutch also built the nearby **Christ Church**, which retains much of its original seating. On the hill to the rear stands the ruined **St Paul's Church**. This dates from 1521, when the Portuguese were in control. It is worth making the climb to the top if only for the view over the Straits of Melaka. A now empty grave once contained the body of Francisco Xavier who worked as a missionary in the town. His remains were later taken to India. The path down the other side of the hill leads to **Porta de Santiago**, a huge stone gateway that is all that remains from the Portuguese fortress known as 'A Famosa' (1511). The **Cheng Hoon Teng Temple**, Malaysia's oldest Buddhist temple (1645) stands on the other side of the Melaka River.

Part of the colonial heritage

There are tours to Melaka from Singapore, but the journey time prevents travellers doing justice to all the sights or having a good wander round the excellent antique shops (e.g. Jl. Hang Jebat). Sightseeing Tour East, 3C River Valley Road, Clarke Quay (#01-24/25 Cannery Block), tel: 332 3755. It is worth staying for two or three days if time permits. The commendable **Melaka Village Park Plaza Resort** ($$$) is about 10 minutes' drive from Melaka in a peaceful spot by a lake. Tel: 06/323600, fax: 325955.

Cheng Hoon Teng Temple detail

Batam Island

The ferry to Batam takes around 30 minutes. Regular ferry services leave from the World Trade Centre every half hour 7.30am–7pm. Tourism has brought rapid changes to Batam and the island is now a supply base for the offshore oil industry. Yet lush vegetation and unspoilt settlements still remain. The island is very popular with golfers from Singapore, but the loveliest attraction here is the Nongsa beach. The Turi Beach Resort, with Balinese-style cottages facing the sea, is the perfect getaway. Call their Singapore office on 438 0321 for a reservation.

Bintan Island

Bintan, the largest island in the Riau chain, is nearly three times the size of Singapore. Most of the island is made up of thick jungle, swamp and mountains with isolated pockets of people living in villages. But like Batam, tourism has made an impact, at least in the coastal areas. The entire northern coast with its white sandy beaches and clear water has been developed into a mega tourist area called Bintan Resorts. Accommodation ranges from the luxurious Banyan Tree Bintan (tel: 849 5899) and Club Med Ria Bintan (tel: 738 4222), to the de luxe Hotel Sedona Bintan Lagoon (tel: 227 7375) and the Nirwana Garden Resort Hotel (tel: 372 1308 or 1800-323 6636). Ferry services to Bintan leave Singapore from the Tanah Merah Ferry Terminal (TMFT) regularly and the journey takes about 45 minutes.

Art and Customs

Opposite: Chinese and Hindu temples side by side

The racial mix of Chinese, Malay and Indian determines the culture of the city-state. The most impressive buildings are either the temples belonging to the different faiths or the monumental edifices from the colonial era. Singapore's house facades no longer follow the traditional Asian models, as the planners and architects have sought to give the city a thoroughly modern look. Steel, concrete, glass and chrome have replaced the old houses. Where tourism has kept the old shophouses intact, the lines of streets often look drab and sterile. Instead of a full facelift, old walls have simply been smartened up with new ones. Soon the traditional craftsmen, such as woodcarvers, dyers, potters and goldsmiths, will be driven out of existence as their tiny workshops in houses renovated by the state become too expensive.

So Singaporean culture finds expression less in its old buildings and more in its ancient customs and colourful ethnic festivals.

Lighted lanterns at the Mooncake Festival

63

The Malays

Until recently mixed marriages between Moslems and other faiths were the exception. In accordance with ancient traditions, weddings last three days, an occasion when silk and brocade costumes are paraded. Of more importance than the happy couple is the *mak andam*, the woman who organises the expensive spectacle and exhausting banquet. She will be responsible for the wedding garments (six different costumes for both the bride and bridegroom is not exceptional), the complicated makeup and the correct course of the wedding rituals.

Malay ladies in their baju kurung

A Malay family name lasts for little more than one generation, as children always add the name of their father to their own. Sometimes the words 'bin' or 'binte' are placed between first and family names, meaning 'son of' or 'daughter of'.

The natural warmth and hospitality of the Malays is overwhelming. Foreigners should, however, be aware of certain taboos: men should not touch women (and vice versa) and revealing clothing is generally frowned upon. Most Malay women in Singapore do not bother with the veil, but in the Geylang Serai and Kampong Glam quarters, it is common to see women wearing the *tudung*, a cloth that covers the hair and neck. Some men wear the *sarung*, a long skirt that is draped around the hips.

The Indians

Brightly coloured saris, the fabric interwoven with gold thread, stand out in the dusty streets of Little India (*see pages 38–41*), but many women also wear the Punjabi dress of northern India: a knee-length shirt over long trousers. The women's gold jewellery is also impossible to miss. Chains and bracelets are the traditional wedding gifts of Indian husbands and goldsmiths' shop windows are invariably surrounded by young women. Only widows leave their jewellery at home.

Out shopping

Many marriages are still arranged by parents and a married woman can be identified by the dab of red powder along the centre parting or by a red spot on the forehead, although this can also be an adornment worn by an unmarried woman. Family names are not usual. Usually, the son adds his father's final name to his own or else places the initial letter of his father's name before his own. Women adopt their husband's name upon marriage.

Almost everything is done with the right hand, whether it is eating, handing over a present or simply returning change. The left, 'unclean' hand is used for bodily hygiene. As for relations with the opposite sex, men should keep at least an arm's length from women in public.

Hindu temple detail

Hindu temples

No one may enter a Hindu temple wearing shoes. But before going inside the building, take a look at the *gopuram*, the colourful gate tower with statues of the deities – Walt Disney would have approved! These images of gods, piled one on top of the other, are typical of the temples of southern India. Even inside, illustrations and representations of the complex world of Hindu gods abound. Centrally positioned and in a lavishly decorated shrine stands the god to whom the temple is dedicated – and he will be guarded by other statues. Sometimes the sacred section of the temple is partitioned off with bars or curtains.

Devotees will present the statue with sacrificial offerings such as garlands, bright metals or opened coconuts whose white flesh symbolises purity. People are always coming and going. The followers who prostrate themselves on the floor are giving themselves unconditionally to their god. The brahman, as the Hindu priest is called, is the medium between god and his devotees. He has many often complicated rituals to perform, especially during the regular temple festivals.

The Chinese

The Chinese love to show others what they have and what they are. The 'yuppie' sons and daughters of the rich have simple tastes – only the best will do. Whether it is clothing, music, theatre, a car or a flat, for the young Chinese of Singapore it must be Western. Even a Western first name is essential. The boy given the name Tan Yock Suan (Tan is by far the most common surname), will probably be referred to as Paul Tan. Only the older generation still live in the traditional two- or three-storey shophouses – that is, shop on the ground floor, living quarters upstairs.

By contrast, *Wayang*, better known to foreigners as Chinese opera, is pure, unadulterated China. This traditional musical theatre – *wayang* comes from Malay and means 'play' – is performed on simple stages in all parts of Singapore. Its monotonous rhythms and clanging cymbals are not always to Westerners' taste, but it is certainly fascinating to watch the actors in their colourful costumes and with their faces made up to signify the age, status, views and morality of the character they are depicting. The simple plots are derived from ancient Chinese legends, myths and history.

Chinese temples

It is easy to gain the impression that a Chinese temple is no different from a market place. Everyone chatters and laughs, families unwrap their food, mothers scold their unruly children and the toilet gets flushed. But is there any room for reverence?

65

Despite appearances, there is. It involves the faithful lighting their three incense sticks (symbolising past, present and future) and holding them up in ardent prayer; and it involves them sharing a meal with the dead in front of a memorial plaque to their ancestors. Religion is a kind of game that believers play with the countless temple gods. The rules are: 'You give to me and I will give to you'. Offerings are given in return for advice, which the temple guard even writes down. Another popular trade-off involves the statues of the two 'penitent players'. Hanging round their necks are bags containing tips for the forthcoming lottery. Of course, any winners must share their prizes with the tipsters.

Chinese devotee and temple

Chinese Opera

Offerings to the Monkey God
Lion guard

The Chinese assign a different responsibility to each of their gods and goddesses and so there are many different statues in Chinese temples. Buddha is one of them, but others include the god of war, the Monkey God and the emperor's gods, not forgetting the guards and the spirits from the mythological world. A lion and lioness traditionally protect the entrance, but people have little confidence in their vigilance and erect knee-high barriers as well, to trip up any evil spirits.

Feng shui

Anyone who dreads encountering a black cat will understand about *feng shui*, but the Chinese would be appalled if *feng shui* were to be equated with superstition. For the Chinese, *feng shui* (meaning 'wind and water') is a science, based on the Taoist concept of *yin* and *yang*, although it is accepted that demons and spirits also play their part. In practice, important events in a person's life, such as marriage, birth of children, the construction of a new house and their funeral must be conducted according to certain rules so that harmony with nature is not destroyed. Evil influences and spirits must be warded off. That is why the Chinese build the entrance to their houses away from the street, otherwise the spirits would have easy access to the interior. A mirror attached to the front of the house helps to keep evil spirits away. Even modern housebuilders pay heed to *feng shui*. If a business does not prosper, then something is probably wrong with the *feng shui*. A waterfall by the entrance (which will stop the money flowing away) can sometimes work wonders.

To make absolutely certain that things are right, a geomancy expert may have to be called in. One of the most famous and best-paid geomancy specialists is called Master Tan. He will also know what a child should be called and will be able to predict the child's future according to the Chinese horoscope. His office is open to the public and visitors can find out more about *feng shui* there (Mon–Fri, 10am–7pm). Master Tan, Way Chinese Geomancy Pte Ltd, 149 Rochor Road (Fu Lu Shou Complex, near Bugis Street, #02-11), tel: 336 3060.

Literature

In the first half of the 20th century, important Western literary figures such as Joseph Conrad, Somerset Maugham and Rudyard Kipling were colourful players in the island's colonial life, and their accounts – often centred on the Raffles Hotel *(see pages 26 and 77)* – provide an insight into the way rich Western settlers lived in Singapore. The writings of modern Singaporean authors such as Tan Kok Seng and Catherine Lim deal with the day-to-day problems of life in the growing city-state.

Festivals

Few other countries in the world can offer so many festivals all year round. Whatever the time of year, someone somewhere in Singapore is sure to be celebrating. Here is a selection of the main events:

The **Chinese New Year** (Lunar New Year, January/February) is an occasion for merry-making that lasts for two weeks. The lion and dragon dances and the Chingay Parade of musicians, acrobats and dancers are the highlights. The first two days are official holidays and many of the streets and squares are decorated with coloured lights, oil lamps and *papier-mâché* figures.

By New Year's Day, houses and flats must be cleaned and all debts paid and, from then on, a new creature from the Chinese astrological year influences fortunes. Envelopes with money *(hong bao)* – or at least symbolic money – are distributed and guests present their hosts with mandarin oranges as presents.

Thaipusam (January/February), which takes place at a specific phase of the moon, is a day of repentance for Hindus. A macabre highlight occurs in the afternoon when the devotees torture themselves by piercing skewers and metal spikes into their bodies and then walk the 3km (2 miles) from Sri Srinivasa Perumal Temple in Serangoon Road to the Sri Thandayuthapani Temple (sometimes known as Chettiar Temple) in Tank Road.

Birthday of the Monkey God (February/March and September/October) is celebrated by the Chinese twice a year. During the celebrations, the spirit of the Monkey God enters into mediums, who skewer their cheeks and tongues with spikes and write charms in their own blood.

Monkey God birthday celebration

Ramadan (dates change annually), the month when Moslems fast, is the best time of year to sample Malay delicacies. Around the Sultan Mosque (*see page 43*), numerous snack bars wait to sell tasty offerings as the hungry believers are only allowed to eat after sunset. Ramadan ends with a grand festival, the **Hari Raya Puasa**, when friends and family meet for a lavish meal.

The **Qing Ming Festival** (April) is the Chinese equivalent of All Souls' Day. The Chinese decorate the graves of their ancestors and take food and other offerings to the cemeteries.

Hari Raya Haji (dates change annually) is a day which Moslems spend in prayer, while remembering those who

Buddha and a follower

are making a pilgrimage to Mecca. Animals are slaughtered in the late afternoon near the Sultan Mosque and the meat is then distributed to the needy.

Vesak Day (May) is a sacred day for Buddhists. It is the day when devout Buddhists celebrate the birth, enlightenment and death of Buddha with fervent prayer and by making offerings in the temples (e.g. Temple of the Thousand Lights, *see page 41*). The festival begins with traditional chants and then birds are released from their cages, a gesture that Buddhists hope will bring salvation. A candle-lit procession concludes the day.

The **Dragon Boat Festival** (June) consists mainly of a boat race in which participants from all over the world take part. The event is dedicated to the Chinese poet and statesman Qu Yuan. Over 2,500 years ago, he drowned himself in protest against corruption and injustice. According to legend, fishermen rushed into the water to save him and by beating drums and thrashing the water they stopped the fish from devouring him. In today's races, the sound of wild drumbeats precedes the racing boats.

The **Singapore Food Festival** (1–31 July) allows food lovers to indulge themselves in a way unimaginable at other times of the year. Gourmets are invited to sample new dishes that restaurant chefs have devised.

At the **Festival of the Hungry Ghost** (July/August) a feast is provided for the hungry spirits of dead Chinese. Throughout the city, food is left in bowls for the dead. The financial needs of the dead are also met by providing imitation bank notes and credit cards. The living enjoy themselves by watching one of the Chinese operas that are performed in Chinatown and on many of the estates, sometimes twice a day.

National Day (9 August), celebrating independence, appeals to the patriotism of Singaporeans. Folk groups, schools, music groups, social clubs and the military all take part in parades in the Padang or national stadium (*see page 23*). You need tickets, which are always in short supply. A laser and firework display ends the day.

The **Mooncake Festival** (September/October at the time of the full moon) recalls the victory of the Chinese over the Mongols courtesy of Zhu Yuan Zhang, who outwitted the hated occupying forces with messages hidden in little cakes. Children parade with lanterns and everyone eats pastries filled with lotus seeds, red bean paste and salted egg yolk.

Navarathiri (September/October) is Tamil for *nine nights*. This festival honours supreme goddess Devi with three nights devoted to each incarnation: Durga, Lakshmi and Saraswathi. You can hear classical Indian music and watch traditional dancing. The Chettiar Temple in Tank Road is a good place to see the performances (*see page 55*).

Thimithi (September/October) is a Hindu festival in honour of the goddess Draupadai. At the Sri Mariamman Temple (*see page 32*) men run barefoot across glowing embers. For a good view, it is best to arrive early.

Pilgrimage to Kusu Island (September/October/November). Chinese Taoists pay their respects at the Tua Pekong Temple on the island of Kusu where legend says a giant turtle saved a shipwrecked Malay and Chinese from drowning by turning itself into the island.

Deepavali (October/November), or the Festival of Lights, celebrates the victory of light over darkness. Serangoon Road is the focal point for the festivities. Garlands brighten Little India by day and illuminations by night. Restaurants and food stalls serve special delicacies.

Deepavali illuminations

The **Festival of the Nine Emperor Gods** (October/November) lasts nine days. Colourful processions and Chinese opera honour the gods so they will heal the sick and grant long life. The Kiu Ong Yiah Temple in Upper Serangoon Road is at the centre of the festivities.

Christmas lights (November to January) brighten Orchard Road for weeks, and hotels and shopping centres compete for best decorated building. Few Singaporeans confess to being Christian, but many are crazy about Christmas and giving presents is an accepted custom.

Mooncake Festival magic

Food and Drink

A fact always well understood by lovers of fine food has now been recognised by tourists: Singapore has many culinary attractions. In the multiracial melting pot, all the various cuisines compete in the battle of the taste buds: Chinese, Indonesian, Malaysian, Indian, Thai, Japanese, Korean, Arab. The choice is further complicated because Hokkien Chinese cooking is quite different from Cantonese, and southern Indians like their food hotter than their countrymen further north.

The choice of restaurants is vast, and even dyed-in-the-wool consumers of European food will not be disappointed. Pasta and pizza parlours abound, alongside French *haute cuisine* restaurants and burger bars. It is easy to eat well and cheaply in Singapore. In every shopping centre stalls serve quick food at a reasonable price.

Dining and drinking

The prices of meals in the restaurants of luxury hotels are on a par with international levels, but alcohol, particularly wine, will push the price up quite dramatically. Even a bottle of the local beer (Anchor, Tiger) – certainly as good as an imported beer – will add about six dollars to the bill. To save money, do what the Singaporeans do and drink water or tea. Both are usually provided free of charge with the meal.

Three important tips: 'hot' means really hot, 'spicy' is milder, but still hot; smoking is forbidden in air-conditioned restaurants (and pubs that serve food); 14 percent is added for service and tax; waiters do not expect a tip.

The descriptions of the various cuisines that follow include recommendations for relevant speciality restaurants, listed according to three categories: $$$ = expensive; $$ = moderate; $ = inexpensive.

Nonya

Nonya cooking grew out of the first Chinese-Malay marriages. The menfolk did not wish to give up their favourite dishes and certainly not pork, which is excluded from all Malay recipes because of Moslem rules. Nonya food usually consists of Chinese ingredients, such as vegetables, meat and fish, which are then prepared in the Malay style, often with chilli and coconut milk. *Otak-otak*, a dish in which fish is wrapped in a banana leaf, is prepared in the typical Malay fashion and, generally, the food is hot and spicy with a high calorie count. Coconut milk and sugar are certainly not spared in the preparation of desserts. Unfortunately, only a few restaurants serve Nonya food.
$$**Chilli Padi Nonya Family Restaurant**, 6 Kim Tian Road, tel: 275 1001. $$**Peranakan Inn**, 210 East Coast Road, tel: 440 6195.

71

Chinese

Don't be surprised if a Chinese greets you with 'Have you eaten?' and not 'How are you?' To say that you have a full stomach is like saying 'I'm fine'. For the Chinese, eating is probably the most important thing in the world. In the words of an old Chinese proverb: 'Everything that moves with its back to the sun is edible'.

Most people will recognise the items on Chinese menus: spring rolls or prawn noodle soup for starters, followed perhaps by Peking duck, served with bean sprouts and fried rice. The dessert menu will almost certainly include banana fritters. To be a little more adventurous try shark's fin soup, chilli crab or bird's nest. Eating a bird's nest may seem unattractive, but what is eaten is the bird's hardened, glue-like saliva that binds the nest. Before eating, all leaves and grasses are removed. The rather bland taste in no way justifies the huge price (up to S$150 per portion).

Snacks in the market

On two matters all Chinese agree. It is improper to gesticulate with chopsticks or point them at anyone and rice or noodles form an essential part of any meal. After that, the tastes of the various Chinese regions drift apart. Nearly all of them are represented, even though most of the Chinese in Singapore originate from the southern provinces.

Hokkien

The largest dialect group has very little to boast about in gastronomic terms, and few restaurants serve Hokkien cuisine. Pork is popular – with plenty of fat. Hokkien Chinese like rich, satisfying food. Soups are served with vegetables and meatballs. Fried *hokkien mee* – a wholesome noodle dish with vegetables, meat, fish and garlic in a creamy sauce – is popular. It is the unofficial national dish of Singapore and can be enjoyed at many food stalls.
$$–$$$Beng Thin Hoon Kee, OCBC Centre (5th floor), 65 Chulia Street, tel: 533 7708. **$$Beng Hiang**, 112 Amoy Street, tel: 221 6684.

Cantonese

Cantonese is many people's favourite – perhaps because it is always elegantly presented, as, for example, in Hong Kong, where the exquisite 'little hearts' *(dim sum)*, traditional gifts given 'from the heart', are served for lunch. Shark's fin soup is another famous Cantonese dish. Wealthier inhabitants of the old province of Canton did not eat to build up their strength for work in the fields, they ate for enjoyment, so the food is often light with delicate and imaginative spice mixtures, which bring out the full natural aroma of the ingredients – meat and seafood in particular.
$$$Hung Kang Restaurant, 38 North Canal Road, tel: 533 5300. The best place for shark's fin soup. **$$–$$$Mitzi**

Cantonese Restaurant, 24/26 Murray Street, tel: 222 8281. **$$–$$$ Wang Jiang Lou**, Clarke Quay (Merchants Court, #01-09), tel: 338 3001. **$$Lee Tong Kee**, 278 South Bridge Road (near Sago Street), tel: 223 1896. Well known for its dim sum and noodle soups.

Variety is the spice of life

Teochew

The recipes of the second-largest dialect group concentrate on lighter, easily digestible foods. Many Teochew Chinese earned their living from fishing, so the dishes tend to be mainly seafood. Particularly popular are the fish balls made from finely chopped fish, salt and water that are added to soups and noodles. Another Teochew speciality which all Singaporeans enjoy for breakfast is a kind of porridge made from fish, meat or vegetables.
$$Teochew Garden, United Square #01–52, tel: 255 6636. **$–$$Ban Seng**, 79 New Bridge Road, tel: 533 1471.

Hakka

Hakka food can be described as simple and undemanding, just like the lives of the old Hakka nomads in China. Soya bean yoghurt often replaces meat and, instead of fresh vegetables, ingredients preserved in salt are added to many dishes. Nevertheless, the rather basic food is still very tasty. Try *yong tau foo*, a soya bean yoghurt with chopped meat.
$–$$Moi Kong, 22 Murray Street, tel: 221 7758.

Basic food can be very tasty

Sichuan

For centuries, strong spices have been used in the western province of China. Chilli, the stronger the better, has always been a favourite, but take care with the dried, red chillies that can burn the tongue and cause considerable discomfort. Try one of the typical fried dishes with chicken or prawns served with whole, dried chilli pods.
$$$Min Jiang (in Goodwood Park Hotel), 22 Scotts Road, tel: 737 5337. **$$–$$$Dragon City**, 214 Dunearn Road (Novotel Orchid), tel: 254 5477.

Beijing

The delicious crispy skin of the Peking Duck, rolled in thin pancakes with a sweet bean sauce and spring onions, is a famous Beijing speciality, usually served as an appetiser. The duck meat and vegetables follow as the second course. Only then is the duck soup served. But duck is not the only meat on offer. Excellent lamb and mutton dishes are also very popular. These were introduced to Beijing many years ago by Moslems from neighbouring Mongolia and Manchuria.
$$–$$$Pine Court, Orchard Road (Mandarin Hotel, 36th floor), tel: 831 6262. **$$$Chang Jiang** (in Goodwood Park Hotel), 22 Scotts Road, tel: 737 7411.

Hainan

It is said that Hainan has borrowed heavily from Western cooking. Chicken rice, for example, involves cooking the fowl slowly and then adding rice to the stock. A chilli-garlic sauce gives extra flavour. The Hainan invented the steamboat, a type of fondue where everyone cooks their food in a communal pot filled with stock. When ready, the morsels are dipped in various sauces.

Fresh greens

$$–$$$Charming Garden (in the Novotel Orchid), 214 Dunearn Road, tel: 251 8149. **$Mooi Chin**, Funan Centre #01-05, tel: 339 7766.

Herbal

The Chinese live to eat, so they take their food very seriously. The effect of certain food and food combinations have been studied in China for centuries. The concern of many cooks is to create a balanced diet, so that the *yin* (cooling) and *yang* (warming) balance the body. Such a diet will also taste good, but that is a pleasant side effect. It is not easy for the layman to tell *yin* from *yang* foods and know which herbs have healing powers.

$$$Imperial Herbal Restaurant (in the Metropole Hotel), 41 Seah Street, tel: 337 0491.

Vegetarian

A diet without meat might seem to suit the Chinese preoccupation with food and health but, apart from strict Buddhists, few Chinese are vegetarians. One reason may be that Chinese shun raw food, although soya-bean yoghurt and other vegetarians' favourites form part of the Chinese diet. Nevertheless, there are many restaurants (some Indian) that prepare imaginative vegetarian dishes.

$$–$$$Bombay-Woodlands, Tanglin Road (Tanglin Shopping Centre), tel: 235 2712. **$$Kamats**, 102 Serangoon Road, tel: 291 7930 (Indian/vegetarian). **$$Fut Sai Kai**, 147 Kitchener Road, tel: 298 0336. **$$Loke Woh Yuen Vegetarian Restaurant**, 20 Tanjong Pagar Road, tel: 221 2912.

Seafood

Singapore is an island, so fresh fish and seafood have always played an important part in the native diet. Nowadays, what is not available close at hand is imported, e.g. large crabs from Sri Lanka and giant lobsters from Thailand. Most of the seafood restaurants are concentrated around the East Coast Parkway.

Seafood is everywhere

Fish and crustaceans are usually boiled or grilled. Drunken prawns is a macabre dish where the live prawns are brought to the table in a bowl of alcohol. When the little creatures are 'drunk', the spirit is lit. Far more appetising is chilli crab – the large crabs are coated in a creamy, fiery-hot sauce. Crispy, fried baby squid served with a dark soya relish is another delicious speciality. **$$$Seafood International Market and Restaurant**, tel: 345 1211. **$UDMC East Coast Seafood Centre**, East Coast Parkway, several outlets (*see Route 8, page 52*). **$$–$$$Long Beach Seafood**, East Coast Parkway, tel: 445 8833, and Planet Marina, #01-01 31 Marina Park, tel: 323 2222. **$$New Kheng Luck**, tel: 442 7909. **$$Palm Beach Seafood**, Lallang Leisure Park, tel: 344 3088.

UDMC Seafood Centre

Malay and Indonesian

Malays have skilfully combined the cooking methods of their northern and southern neighbours, the Thais and the Indonesians. Many dishes are enriched with thick coconut milk sauces or hot chillies. Lemongrass and curry also play a part in Malay cuisine as do coriander and meat. Fish is as popular as meat and chicken, but devout Moslems will not eat pork. *Satays*, small kebabs of marinated meat, are very popular, especially when grilled over charcoal and served with a spicy peanut sauce. Malays and Indonesians do not use chopsticks.

Geylang Serai Market

Malay
$Victory Restaurant, 701 North Bridge Road, tel: 298 6955. **$$–$$$House of Sundanese Food**, 55 Boat Quay, tel: 534 3775 (closed Sunday), Fountain Terrace of Suntec City Mall, tel: 334 1012, and 218 East Coast Road, tel: 345 5020 (closed Monday).
Indonesian
$$The Rice Table, 360 Orchard Road, 02-09/10 International Building, tel: 835 3783, tel: 466 4311. **$–$$Sanur Indonesian**, Orchard Road (Centrepoint Shopping Centre 04–17), tel: 734 2192. **$$Kenari Indonesian**, 409 River Valley Road, tel: 836 0073.

Indian

South Indian food, the sort more likely to be encountered in Singapore, is much hotter than North Indian food. Some dishes may be too hot for Western palates, in which case ask for a mild main course. Yoghurt accompanies most meals and can help tone down spiciness.

Southern Indian dishes usually come with rice; in the north, more bread is eaten. The *roti prata* or soft pancakes from the south are quite delicious for breakfast, but *chapatis* and *naans* from the north accompany all meals. *Dosai* are south Indian specialities, shaped from rice dough and filled with curries.

Southern Indian curries are enriched with coconut milk and are consequently thicker than northern curries. Fish head curry is a Singaporean creation and should not be missed. North Indians often use the clay *tandoor* oven for cooking meat, chicken and fish, and tandoori chicken is very popular. Also worth a try is *jeenga tandoori dil-bahar*, marinated prawns baked in the *tandoor*.

South Indian

$–$$Banana Leaf Apollo, 56 Race Course Road, tel: 293 8682. **$$–$$$Muthu's Curry Restaurant**, 78 Race Course Road, tel: 293 2389. **$$Komala Vilas**, 76 Serangoon Road, tel: 293 6980. **$$–$$$Madras New Woodlands**, 12–14 Upper Dickson Road, tel: 297 1594. **$$Annalakshmi**, 5 Coleman Street (Excelsior Hotel, #02-10), tel: 339 9993. **$–$$Zam Zam**, 699 North Bridge Road (corner of Arab Street), tel: 298 7011.

Shopping for fresh ingredients

North Indian

$$The Tandoor, 11 Cavenagh Road (Holiday Inn Park View basement), tel: 733 8333. **$$Delhi Restaurant**, 60 Race Course Road, tel: 296 4585. **$$Moti Mahal**, 18 Murray Street (Food Alley), tel: 221 4338. **$$–$$$Orchard Maharajah**, 25 Cuppage Terrace, tel: 732 6331 (also al fresco). **$$Kinara**, 57 Boat Quay, tel: 533 0412.

Other Asian cuisines

Almost every nation on the Asian continent is represented in Singapore. Many wealthy Japanese visit the island, so there is now an abundance of *sushi* bars and *teppanyaki* restaurants. These traditional Japanese foods will cost much less than in Tokyo or Osaka and the raw fish that is used in Singapore will also be much fresher. *Sushi* has recently caught on in Singapore and now lots of fast food stalls specialise in these dainty little rolls as well as more traditional Japanese fare such as noodle soup.

Japanese

$$$Unkai, ANA Hotel, 16 Nassim Hill, tel: 732 1222. **$$Hoshigaoka**, 435 Orchard Road (Wisma Atria Shopping Centre, #01-18), tel: 734 2546. Economical family restaurant with accessible menu. **$Genki Sushi**, 16 Collyer Quay, tel: 538 0970, also at 583 Orchard Road, tel: 734 2513. Conveyor-belt sushi.

Thai

$$Lemongrass, 260 Orchard Road (The Heeren, #05-02A), tel: 736 1998. An above-average restaurant with reasonably priced dishes. **$$Bann Thai Restaurant**, Ngee Ann City, Tower A, #04–23, tel: 735 5563.

International

Almost all large hotels have restaurants serving Western food. These establishments often attract tourists bemused by the wealth of foods on offer. Given the wide choice of good-quality ingredients available in Singapore, it is easy for Western chefs to serve up the juicy steaks, fresh vegetables and delicate fish dishes much loved by Europeans and Americans.

Noteworthy restaurants include; **Morton's of Chicago** at the Oriental Hotel; **The Gordon Grill** at the Goodwood Park Hotel; **Harbour Grill & Oyster Bar** at the Hilton International Hotel; **Ristorante Bologna** at the Marina Mandarin Hotel; **L'Aigle d'Or** at the Duxton Hotel; **mezza9** at the Grand Hyatt; and **Prego** at The Westin Plaza. **Alkaff Mansion** is also well known for its *rijstaffel* (*see Further Sights, page 55*).

Alkaff Mansion restaurant

Raffles

Staying in the Raffles Hotel may be out of reach for many tourists, but eating there is a different matter. Two restaurants, the French-style **Raffles Grill** and the Asian **Tiffin Room**, are in the main hotel wing, but four other restaurants are located in the white-painted, two-storey arcade of the exclusive shopping centre: the elegant **Empress Room** serving Cantonese food, **Ah Teng's Bakery** for baguettes, croissants and banana cakes served with cappuccino or jasmin tea, the **Seah Street Deli**, an American-inspired meeting place serving ready-to-eat snacks and meals and finally the **Empire Café** where Singaporean dishes are available. **Raffles Courtyard** is a great place for a late-afternoon drink, while lunch in the **Bar and Billiard Room** can be a lavish affair. In the evening, try a Singapore Sling in the **Long Bar**.

Singapore Sling

This famous drink was first prepared in 1915 by Ngiam Tong Boon, a barman in the original Raffles Hotel. It tastes dangerously fruity and first timers may be lulled into thinking that it contains no alcohol. But that is certainly not the case. The recipe is no longer a secret: 5cl gin, 3cl pineapple juice, 1cl fresh lemon juice, a shot of Benedictine, a shot of Cointreau, and a little cherry brandy. Shake well with ice and then pour into a long glass half-full of ice. Top up with soda water and decorate with fruit. Cheers!

The durian fruit

Many of the tropical fruit available in Singapore give off a pleasant aroma, but the durian fruit stinks to high heaven. For the locals though, it is the 'king of fruits'. Beneath the spiny, browny-green skin, this tree fruit, which is as big as a rugby ball, actually contains some delicious, soft, white flesh. Many tourists hold their noses when they pass the market stalls selling durian, but the Singaporeans will give them a good sniff. It is important to check that the fruit is fully ripe. Good durian fruit are really filling, but their taste is difficult to describe. It is perhaps the creamy

The 'king of fruits'

texture that is so appealing. Anyone wishing to sample without buying can do so at the Four Seasons by Clarke Quay. Taking durians home as a souvenir is definitely not recommended as they are banned by all hotels, all airlines and by the public transport authorities.

Hawker centres

Sometimes called hawkers, these mobile food stands started out selling snacks from the roadside. Over the years, and with a little encouragement from the government, they formed into hawker centres and they have since

Hawker centres, a cheap option

become Singapore's favourite (and cheapest) source of fast food. It is hard to imagine how Singaporeans could survive without the hawker centres. Children eat there at the end of school, and their parents come when they have finished work. Every type of Asian food is available, and that means practically anything that can be prepared quickly – all at incredibly low prices. Choices include char-grilled *satays*, Indian mutton soup from a large pot or wok-fried Hong Kong noodles.

Lau Pa Sat mural

Try **Lau Pa Sat Festival Market** in the heart of the business quarter (Shenton Way/Boon Tat Street), one of the shopping centres in Orchard Road or in Chinatown (e.g. opposite Murray Terrace on Maxwell Road). There is a highly recommended hawker centre on Sentosa Island too.

Popular restaurant quarters

Food Alley (Murray Terrace) in Chinatown is a safer bet than the **Bugis quarter**, where the restaurants and small hawker stalls are rather mediocre in quality. By far the best choice of Asian and European restaurants is by the **Boat Quay** (between Cavanagh Bridge and South Bridge Road). Beware of the 'Wine and Dine Passport' – it bestows no price reductions on the user and only narrows the choice.

At **Clarke Quay** you may like to try: **$$$J.P. Bastiani Mediterranean Bar & Restaurant** (Merchant's Court, tel: 433 0156), with a good Italian menu and a pleasant atmosphere; also **$$$Key Largo Oyster Bar and Seafood Restaurant** (Trader's Market, tel: 334 40 55). In the **$$Steam Boat Restaurant** (Merchant's Court, no reservations) you prepare your own meal al fresco. The **Four Seasons** (Trader's Market) is a good place to try durians. Try hot stone meals, e.g. steaks served on hot stone, on the **Tongkangs** (old cargo boats).

For those who prefer not to stray too far from Orchard Road, **Cuppage Terrace** offers the best in outdoor dining. There is also a good selection of restaurants in the **Ngee Ann City Shopping Centre** (Orchard Road).

Shopping

Orchard Road is still Singapore's main shopping street, but it is worth making a detour into Scotts Road and Tanglin Road (*see Route 2, pages 30-1*). Prices drop a little after Chinese New Year in February, and all shops take part in the Great Singapore Sale in July and August. Most shops are open Monday to Saturday 9.30am–9pm. Shops open on Sunday on Orchard Road.

Tanglin Mall

Shopping tips

In the markets and some shopping centres (e.g. Lucky Plaza on Orchard Road and in Chinatown) haggling is accepted. In the boutiques and department stores along Orchard Road, however, you pay the fixed price. Shops with merlion stickers are members of the city-run Good Retailer Scheme (GRS).

GST (goods and service tax) at 3 percent is added, but if more than S$300 is spent in one shop displaying the tax refund logo, ask for a refund form. Show the goods at a counter in the airport and the GST will be refunded within 12 weeks.

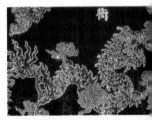

Check that electrical goods will run on your home electricity, and for all electrical goods and cameras make sure the manufacturer's international guarantee card is enclosed (it tends to raise the price a little). If a shop agrees to send an item to your home, obtain written confirmation.

Some trinkets to take home

Visitors can take complaints either to the Singapore Tourist Board (*see page 90*) or the Consumers' Association of Singapore, Bukit Merah Central, Block 164 (#04-3625), tel: 375 8056/270 5433, fax: 270 6786). If the disputed sum is less than S$2,000, the Small Claims Court (2 Havelock Road #05-00, tel: 435 5937; S$10 fee) will resolve the issue within 48 hours.

Antiques

Katong Antique House, Peter Wee, 208 East Coast Road (tel: 345 8544 for an appointment).

Books

MPH **Stamford/Armenian Street**. Three storeys full of books, plus a café. Daily, 10am–9.30pm.

Select Books, Tanglin Shopping Centre, #03-15. Mon–Sat, 10am–9.30pm. Southeast Asian books.

Borders, Wheelock Place, #01-00. Sun–Thurs 9am–11pm, Fri–Sat 9am–noon). Stocks over 200,000 titles and holds weekly readings.

Kinokuniya Bookstores, Ngee Ann City #03-00. . Daily, 10.30am–9.30pm. This is the largest bookshop in Singapore, and also has branches in Liang Court, River Valley Road and at Bugis Junction.

The Raffles Arcades

Computers
Funan Centre, North Bridge Road, by the Singapore River. Most PCs have American keyboards.

Fashion and accessories
Look along **Orchard Road** and **Tanglin Road** (*see Route 2, pages 27-31*), in the **Raffles Hotel Arcade** and in the **Capitol Building** on Stamford Road.

Hi-fi/audio
Sim Lim Square (corner of Rochor Canal and Bencoolen Street), **Adelphi** (corner of Coleman Road and North Bridge Road) and **Plaza Singapura** (Orchard Road).

Jewellery
The determined haggler may get about S$800 knocked off the price of a S$4,500 Rolex watch at the well-stocked clock and watch shop **Thong Hiap** (141 Middle Road). Fake watches are illegal. For unusual jewellery, try the **Tanglin Shopping Centre** and the **Raffles Hotel Arcades** (very expensive). The **Zhujiao Centre** in Little India (Serangoon Road) has a big selection of gold jewellery. To get gold and other jewellery checked, use the **Singapore Assay Office** (tel: 660 7330, fax: 261 2617).

Made-to-measure tailoring
A tailor given 48 hours can produce a wearer-designed suit. A silk suit will cost US$300–1,000.
Men: **Fashion Tailors Menswear**, #02-01 Orchard Plaza, tel: 734 7206. **Justmen's Shop** (Tanglin Shopping Centre, #01-36), tel: 737 4800.
Women: **Coloc Tailor**, #02-29 Raffles Hotel Arcade, tel: 338 9767. **Miss Ming**, 333 Orchard Road, Mandarin Hotel Shopping Centre, #02–06 and 400 Orchard Road, Orchard Towers (opposite the Hilton), #01–26. Daily, 10am–7pm. One of the best places for Thai silk. **China Silk House**, Tanglin Shopping Centre, #02–11.

Photographic equipment
The **People's Park Complex** and **Chinatown Point** offer reasonable prices. Try also **Lucky Plaza** on Orchard Road, the **Far East Shopping Centre** on Scotts Road and the **Far East Plaza** on Orchard Road. Haggling is acceptable in these shops. **Centrepoint** in Orchard Road and **Peninsula Plaza** on North Bridge Road also have a good selection of shops. **Bally Camera Repairer** (#03-33 Far East Shopping Centre, tel: 737 7006) does camera repairs.

Decorative art at Ming Village

Porcelain
Ming Village, 32 Pandan Road, tel: 265 7711. Daily 9am–5.30pm. Take the 78 bus from Clementi MRT station and

then it is a further 10-minute walk *(see Jurong, page 49)*.

The Cannery (#01–36) by Clarke Quay is a small shop selling Ming porcelain.

Souvenirs

The ground floor of the **Raffles Hotel Arcades** can often supply something out of the ordinary.

Antiques of the Orient, Tanglin Shopping Centre, #02-40, tel: 734 9351. Singapore's largest stockist of antiquarian maps, prints and rare books.

Say Tian Hng Buddha Shop, 35 Neil Road, tel: 221 1042. daily 10am–8pm. Deities and religious artefacts.

Hats and things

The Old Thong Chai Building (Seiwaen Arts Centre), 50 Eu Tong Sen Street. *Objets d'art* in an old hospital.

National Museum Shop, 51 Armenian Street. Tasteful souvenirs, jewellery and books.

Fong Moon Kee, 16 Sago Street, tel: 223 0940. Mon–Sat, 10am–8pm. Huge selection of body oils.

Art House, 198A Telok Ayer Street *(see Route 3, page 34)*, tel: 323 5572. Chinese opera costume hire. You can be dressed, made up and photographed (from S$35).

Lim's Arts & Crafts, 211 Holland Avenue (Holland Shopping Centre).

81

Singapore Philatelic Bureau, 1 Killiney Street (opposite the Orchard Plaza on Orchard Road). An eldorado for stamp collectors.

Tea

Tea Chapter, 9A Neil Road, tel: 226 1175. 11am–11pm. *(see page 36)*. The Tea Chapter can only be entered barefoot; the S$5 entrance fee is subtracted from the price of a drink. **Yixing Xuan Tea House** 25 Neil Road. 11am–11pm. Has a wide range of teas and tea sets.

Shopping centres away from Orchard Road

Chinatown *(see Route 3, pages 32–7)*, **Little India** *(see Route 4, pages 38–41)* and **Arab Street** *(see Route 5, pages 42–3)* are popular shopping areas, together with **Marina Square** by the Marina Mandarin, Pan Pacific, Oriental and Ritz Carlton hotels and **Clarke Quay**.

Arab Street baskets

Explore shophouses by the Singapore River in the afternoon or early evening when the 100 or so shops are open. The **Fu Lu Shou Centre** by Rochor Road (nearest MRT station: Bugis) is popular with locals. A few traders have moved here from nearby Bugis Street.

Markets

The oldest Singapore markets are found in **Geylang Serai** *(see Route 8, pages 50–2)*, **Chinatown** (Chinatown Complex, *see Route 3, pages 32–7)* and **Little India** *(see Route 4, pages 38–41)*.

Nightlife

Singapore's nightlife hit its stride at the beginning of the 1990s. Boat Quay and Clarke Quay were restored and several large discos opened up beside the Singapore River. Now the city pulsates well into the early hours. Eating out and going to discos is not cheap in Singapore. A glass of wine will cost S$7–10 and at weekends expect a cover charge at clubs. Entrance charges vary between S$10–25. Many pubs have a happy hour around 5–8pm.

Most Singaporeans go out only at weekends, so that is when the bars and discos are full and the karaoke bars around Tanjong Pagar come alive. For a quieter, romantic evening, try the interesting Musical Fountains on Sentosa Island (from 7.30pm) or a cruise on a junk around the illuminated harbour with the glittering backdrop of the Singapore skyline (Watertours, tel: 533 9811, daily from 6.30pm, about 2½ hours, dinner included). For the best view of the city at night, visit the **Compass Rose Bar** in the Westin Stamford Hotel (*see page 26*).

There is always a lot happening in **Chinatown** (around Duxton Road/Tanjong Pagar), on **Bugis Street** (night market/restaurants), **Cuppage Terrace** (restaurants and pubs near Orchard Road) or at the **Lau Pa Sat Festival Market**. The **Adventure Ride** on Clarke Quay is a fantastic, ten-minute boat trip Disney-style along an 'artificial' Singapore River (open daily 10am–10pm, 3E River Valley Road, #01–13). An evening stroll along the **Boat Quay** by Singapore River is a relaxing way to end the day.

Ask the hotel reception for the current *This Week Singapore* or look in the *Straits Times*, Singapore's daily newspaper. The tourist office will provide information on evening performances of Chinese opera (*wayang*).

Night lights on Bugis Street

Dinner shows

Singa Inn Seafood Restaurant, 920 East Coast Parkway (by the Big Splash leisure pool), tel: 345 1111. The 40-minute Asian Cultural Show (Mon–Fri, 8pm) is free, but guests must order an à la carte meal.

The best bars

Harry's Quayside Café, 28 Boat Quay, tel: 538 3029. Where the pin-stripe brigade meet for lunch and dinner.

Hard Rock Café, 50 Cuscaden Road, tel: 235 5232. As popular as anywhere else in the world.

Flag & Whistle, 10 Duxton Hill, tel: 223 1126. British pub and restaurant (closed Sunday).

Papa Joe's, Peranakan Place, 180 Orchard Road, tel: 732 6966. A live band gives energetic performances.

Bar & Billiard Room, Raffles Hotel Arcade, 1 Beach Road, tel: 337 1886. Stylish restaurant that has become a refined 'après dinner' meeting-place – with billiard table.

The Long Bar (Raffles Hotel Arcade). Home of the Singapore Sling and the only place in Singapore where there is no fine for throwing litter on the floor.

Elvis Place, 298 Beach Road, The Concourse, Basement 1, #01-13, tel: 299 8403. Elvis souvenirs and 1950s music.

Crazy Elephant, Traders Market, Clarke Quay, tel: 337 1990. A live band plays jazz and blues every evening (except Monday).

Culture Club, Boat Quay, tel: 536 2471. Friendly atmosphere, live music, pool tables and relaxed disco.

Coco Carib, Boat Quay, tel: 435 1801. Popular and laid back venue with Jamaican steel-band and good tapas.

The best discos

Venom, 9 Scotts Road, Pacific Plaza, level 12, tel: 734 7677. A popular spot for the young and flashy.

Nextpage, 17 Mohammed Sultan Road, tel: 235 6967. A favourite spot for expats and professionals, which plays alternative, pop and retro tunes.

Pleasure Dome, 277 Orchard Road, Specialist Shopping Centre, tel: 834 1221. This award-winning disco is very upmarket, attracting mainly executives and yuppies.

Sultan of Swing, #01-02/03 Central Mall, Magazine Road, tel: 557 0828. Reputedly Singapore's largest disco accommodating 2,000 patrons.

Sparks, Level 8, Ngee Ann City, 391 Orchard Road, tel: 732 6133. Another popular dance hall.

Top Ten, 400 Orchard Road, #04–35 Orchard Towers, tel: 732 3077. Once a cinema and now Singapore's most successful disco.

Zouk, Phuture & Velvet Underground, 17, 19 & 21 Jiak Kim Street (corner of Kim Seng Road), tel: 738 2988. Wine bar and disco in an old warehouse. Closed Monday.

83

Tanjong Pagar and Boat Quay

Getting There

Opposite: arriving in Tanjong Pagar

Opinion polls have consistently shown that air travellers rate Changi Airport very highly and with justification. Sometimes referred to as an 'Airtropolis', the terminals here have seen annual passenger numbers rise to over 20 million. The signposting is excellent and it is stated in the regulations that the first piece of luggage must be on the carousel within 12 minutes of a plane's arrival. The airport is equipped with a professional Business Centre (3rd floor, 8.30am–10pm), three post and telephone counters and several banks. Money changing facilities are available immediately on arrival.

At the moment, there are two terminals, linked by a free 'skytrain'. **Singapore Airlines**, one of the most profitable airlines in the world, are based in Terminal 2, together with **American Airlines**, **Royal Brunei Airlines**, **Air New Zealand**, **Austrian Airlines**, **Delta Airlines**, **Finnair**, **Myanmar Airways**, **Swissair**, **Philippine Airlines**, **Air France**, **Silkair** and **Malaysia Airlines**. All other airlines use Terminal 1. Singapore Airlines (SIA) connects Singapore with all the world's major cities.

Two hotels in the airport offer day rooms, for transit passengers only (about S$55 for six hours, tel: 542 5536, Terminal 1, or 542 8122, Terminal 2). Air transit passengers should remember to pack swimming gear in their in-flight luggage, as they are allowed to use the swimming pool in Terminal 1. Open: 7am–8pm, free for hotel guests. Passengers with a stopover wait of more than four hours are entitled to a sightseeing tour of the city (daily, 10.30am, 2.30 and 4.30pm).

Changi Airtropolis

Transfer to the city centre by taxi is never a problem as sufficient taxis are always at hand. The fare is S$20 including S$3 airport supplement. The journey time is about 20 minutes.

An airport tax of S$15 is due for return or onward flights and this can only be paid in the local currency. Some hotels sell the appropriate coupons at reception.

It is essential to confirm return flight times at least 72 hours before departure. This can be done at the appropriate airline office, either in person or by phone. Remember to have the reconfirmation code number to hand.

By sea

Arriving slowly by sea, as everyone was obliged to do in days gone by, is a pleasant experience. You sail in past 600 or so other vessels lying at anchor, watching the skyline clarify into looming skyscrapers. Most visitors arrive at one of the three terminals of the impressive Singapore Cruise Centre, which can accommodate up to 1,000 passengers at a time.

The MRT is spotless

Getting Around

Taxis and the superb public transport system are by far the best way of touring Singapore. The government uses heavy financial penalties to keep private cars off the road.

MRT (Mass Rapid Transit) System

The air-conditioned underground stations are finished in marble, glass, chrome and stone; their interiors are always clean and polished. The network extends for 83km (51 miles) and tickets cost between S$0.70 and S$1.60. Keep the ticket, as it is needed to open and close the barrier at the station entrance and exit.

A tourist ticket can be purchased for S$7. It may not reduce the cost of travelling but it does make a good souvenir. The TransitLink ticket (S$12 including $2 deposit) is valid for the MRT and buses. Both this and the tourist ticket are available from all MRT stations. The cost of each journey is automatically deducted from the card. The MRT operates 6am–midnight.

The first fully automated Light Rapid Transit (LRT) system opened in 1999 at Pasir Panjang, linking it to the Choa Chu Kang MRT Station. More LRT stations are being planned and passengers can look forward to seamless transit across the island in the near future.

Getting ahead

Buses

SBS and TIBS are the main bus companies. The bus route network is dense and services connect every corner of the island. More than half of the buses are air-conditioned, and fares range from S$0.70 to S$1.60. Always keep plenty of change handy or else buy a Singapore Explorer Ticket (available from hotels; S$5 for one day, S$12 for three days; city map showing all bus routes included). The

Singapore Trolley also issues day passes (available from hotels; S\$9). These old-fashioned trams run 9am–5pm at 30-minute intervals and cover all the main sights in the city centre. They stop at WTC for transfer to Sentosa.

Taxis

More than 18,000 taxis use the streets of Singapore; they are only hard to find on Friday and Saturday evenings. The best plan at these times is to wait at a hotel entrance.

The basic charge of S\$2.40 covers the first kilometre; each additional 240m (260 yards) cost 10 cents. Fares rise by 50 percent between midnight and 6am. If the taxi enters the Central Business District (CBD) any time between 7.30am–7pm Mon–Fri, there is a surcharge of S\$0.40 to S\$1.70. If the taxi passes Electronic Road Pricing (ERP) gantry points – a system to reduce traffic flow in the city – any time between 7.30–9.30am Mon–Fri, there is a surcharge of S\$0.40 to S\$1.40. If you hire a taxi within the CBD any time between 4.30–7pm Mon–Fri and 11am–2pm Sat, a surcharge of S\$1.50 applies.

Trishaws

Trishaws are bicycles with sidecars – ideal for taking tourists on sightseeing trips, but impractical as a serious means of transport. Fares must be paid in advance. Expect to pay S\$25–30 per half-hour.

Boats

Wooden *bumboats* leave for boat trips on the Singapore River from the Raffles Landing Stage *(see page 22)* and Chinese junks depart from Clifford Pier for day and night

Trishaws are good for sightseeing

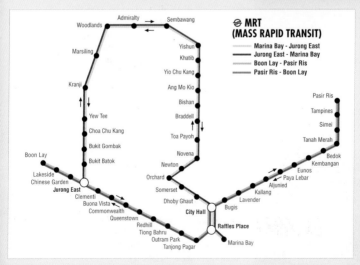

cruises around the harbour (*see page 59*). Boats to Indonesia and the smaller islands leave from the World Trade Centre (WTC). On the second floor of the WTC, a number of travel agents offer stand-by cruises or short trips (with accommodation) to Indonesia.

Sentosa

Entrance to Sentosa is S$5 per person (S$3 for children). There are additional charges for the various attractions within the theme park.

Sentosa can be reached by ferry (S$2.30 for a return trip) from the World Trade Centre (WTC), by cable car from the WTC or Mount Faber (S$6.90 2-way for adult; children below 12 pay S$3.90) or across the causeway on foot or by bus or taxi.

The WTC is served by the Singapore Trolley (*see page 86*); bus Nos 97 or 100 and 10 from Shenton Way (Clifford Pier). Bus A goes from WTC as far as Underwater World. Ferries for the four-minute crossing to Sentosa depart every 20 minutes from the WTC's ground floor, daily 10am–9pm. Every 30 minutes a bus shuttle runs between Sentosa and the WTC.

From Tiong Bahru MRT station, bus C goes to Central Beach (every 10 minutes, Sat–Sun only, 8am–7pm). Bus E leaves departs from the Lucky Plaza shopping centre in Orchard Road.

The last bus leaves Sentosa at 11.30pm. If the taxi queue is too big, take the bus to Tiong Bahru MRT station then go by underground to the city centre and hail a taxi.

To Malaysia and Thailand

You can fly to Malaysia and Thailand from Changi. Anyone planning to rent a car to drive in Malaysia is advised to hire in Johor Bahru (*see Excursions, page 60*), rather than Singapore. To stop 'fuel tourism' the authorities insist tanks in hire cars leaving Singapore must be at least three-quarters full of the more expensive Singaporean fuel.

Several buses a day leave for Johor Bahru or Kuala Lumpur (Pan Malaysia Express Pte, on the corner of Kallang Bahru and Lavender Street, tel: 293 5915). Tickets must be purchased one day in advance.

Singapore does not have railway lines: the station in Keppel Road belongs to Malaysia. Six trains a day leave here for Kuala Lumpur (journey time: approx. 7 hours). Twice a week, the ultra-expensive **Eastern & Orient Express** journeys through jungle and plantations to Bangkok. The 2,030-km (1,262-mile) journey takes about 49 hours. You can reserve seats for part of the journey, tel: 392 3500.

Every day at 8.30am a boat for Tioman in West Malaysia leaves from Tanah Merah Ferry Terminal. Auto Batam Ferries & Tours, tel: 542 7105.

At the E&O

Facts for the Visitor

Visas

Visitors do not need a visa prior to travel to Singapore; they will normally be given a two-week tourist visa on arrival. Those staying longer than 14 days in Singapore can extend their visa by applying to the Immigration Department, 10 Kallang Road, tel: 391 6100. Excursions to Indonesia and Malaysia do not require visas.

Customs

Duty-free goods (except cigarettes) can be bought on arrival in Singapore's Changi airport before passing through customs control. Cigarettes brought into Singapore attract a surcharge of S$17 per carton, regardless of where they were bought. It is possible to leave imported cigarettes with the Singaporean customs authorities and collect them when leaving the country.

Cigarettes may be bought in the airport duty-free shop before leaving. There are no export duties in Singapore and no limits for importing or exporting the Singapore dollar. Chewing gum may not be imported into Singapore, though small amounts for personal use are allowed.

Drug dealers and anyone caught in possession of narcotics face the death penalty under Singapore law.

Travellers over the age of 18 may import 1 litre spirits and 1 litre wine duty-free. Pornographic magazines, videos and weapons (even blowpipes) may not be imported. For details, call the Customs Duty Office at Changi airport, tel: 542 7058 (T1) or 543 0754 (T2).

Under the CITES agreement, the importation into Europe of animal skins, ivory, turtle shell, etc, is banned. If any of these items are found by customs officers, they will be confiscated and a heavy fine can be imposed.

Jungle rock

One for the album

Tourist information

The Singapore Tourism Promotion Board (STB) keeps a large collection of brochures for potential visitors.

In the UK: 1st Floor, Carrington House, 126–130 Regent Street. London W1R 5FE, tel: 44 207 437 0033, fax: 44 207 734 2191; toll free in UK only, tel: 08080 656 565; www.newasia-singapore.com

In the US: 8484 Wilshire Boulevard, Suite 510, Beverly Hills, CA 90211, tel: 213 852 1901, fax: 213 852 0129; 590 Fifth Avenue, 12th Floor, New York, NY 10036, tel: 212 302 4861, fax: 212 302 4801; Two Prudential Plaza, 180 North Stetson Avenue, Suite 2615, Chicago, Illinois 60601, tel: 312 938 1888. US website: www.singapore-usa.com

In Hong Kong: Room 2003 Central Plaza, 18 Harbour Road, Wanchai, tel: 852 2598 9290, fax: 852 2598 1040; www.singapore.com.tw

In Singapore: Tourism Court, 1 Orchard Spring Lane, tel: 736 6622, fax: 736 9423; www.stb.com.sg. Daily, 8.30am–6pm.

Currency and exchange

Singapore's dollar (S$) consists of 100 cents. Money can be changed in banks, hotels and licensed *bureaux de change*. Credit cards are welcomed almost everywhere. It is also useful to take travellers' cheques. These can be changed at the Authorised Money Changers in the shopping centres – although a better rate is sometimes obtained at banks.

If problems arise with credit cards, ring 1 800 732 2244 (American Express); 1 800 225 5225 (Citibank/Visa); 1 800 292 7055 (Diners Club); 336 5277 (Hongkong Bank, MasterCard and Visa). Banks are open Mon–Fri, 10am–3pm and Sat, 9.30–11am.

Public holidays

Details of the main celebrations are given in the section 'Festivals' (*see pages 67–9*). National holidays in Singapore are as follows: 1 January (New Year's Day); end of January/beginning of February (Chinese New Year); March/April (Good Friday); mid-March/beginning of April (Hari Raya Puasa, end of Ramadan); 1 May (Labour Day); 9 August (National Day); November (Deepavali, Hindu festival of light); 25 December (Christmas).

Deepavali decoration

Telephone

Telephone calls are cheap. A three-minute local call from a public call box will cost about 10 cents. To make an international call from a public phone, buy a phonecard from the post office or a telecom outlet. Cards come in denominations of S$2, 5, 10, 20 or 50. Singapore's telecommunications network is of the highest standard. The Com-centre is open around the clock and you can hire a mobile phone for about S$20 per day. For further information, call toll-free 1626.

For international calls from private phones, dial either 001 or 004, followed by 44 for the UK or 1 for the US or Canada. Omit the 0 from the UK area code and then dial the number. To call Singapore from overseas, dial for an international line followed by 65.

To seek operator assistance, tel: 104. For information, tel: 100. For Yellow Pages enquiries, call 777 7777.

Postal services

Of the Singapore Post branches that open daily, the Change Alley (16 Collyer Quay) branch opens at 8am, Killiney Road branch opens at 9am, and both close at 9pm on weekdays and 4.30pm on weekends and public holidays. Most hotels also offer postal services at reception.

A postcard to Europe requires a 50 cent stamp. It will take a few days to arrive.

Guaranteed delivery

Time

Singapore is eight hours ahead of GMT.

Electricity

Electricity is at the UK standard 220V 50Hz.

Clothing

Pack light and loose-fitting clothes, preferably made of cotton, as the heat in Singapore can be oppressive. However, when walking through the city centre, take an extra layer along, as T-shirts and shorts may not be enough inside shops and restaurants, where air-conditioning units are often set to very cool temperatures.

Memories of Britain

Researching itineraries

TAXI STAND FOR 3 TAXIS

Photography

Many shops offer a rapid film development service. Slide films (E6 process) can be developed at Standard Photo (565 MacPherson Road, tel: 282 9122. Mon–Fri, 9am–6pm).

Language

English is understood practically everywhere. Malay, Mandarin and Tamil are the other official languages.

Tipping

Tipping in restaurants or taxis is not normal in Singapore, as a service charge, usually 10 percent, is included in the bill and shown as an extra. If it is not shown, then a tip of 10 percent will be acceptable.

Medical assistance

Medical provision in Singapore is excellent. The names of doctors are listed in the 'Yellow Pages' under 'Medical Practitioners'. Singapore General Hospital is in Outram Road, tel: 222 3322.

Good private insurance is advisable and should provide for every eventuality.

No inoculations are required for Singapore but, if a trip into Malaysia or Indonesia is planned, a course of malaria tablets is recommended.

Water

Singapore's tap water is perfectly drinkable.

Disabled

It is generally quite easy for disabled people to get about in Singapore. The Singapore tourist office will supply a leaflet entitled 'The Physically Disabled Person's Guide to Accessible Places' and this provides information on disabled access to hotels and tourist sites. The Council for Social Services (tel: 336 1544) can give further details.

Emergencies

Call 999 for police, 995 for ambulance and fire brigade.

Security

Singapore is a safe city, even for women travelling alone. Attacks and muggings are rare, but it is still sensible to look after valuables in hotel rooms.

Diplomatic representation

UK: 100 Tanglin Road, tel: 473 9333. Open 8.30am–1pm and 2–5pm Mon–Fri.
US: 27 Napier Road, tel: 476 9100. Open 8.30am–5pm Mon–Fri.

Accommodation

Raffles Hotel

Hotel prices in Singapore are generally very reasonable despite the high occupancy rates. Expect to pay S$140–250 for a comfortable double room in a centrally located hotel. The standard of accommodation in the large hotels is so high that they do not offer de luxe rooms. It is advisable to book a room in advance.

Airline companies such as Singapore Airlines and Qantas offer very competitive stopover deals. Usually included are the transfers to and from the airport and also a sightseeing tour of the city (from US$40 in a good hotel). To book a room on-the-spot may well cost 50 percent more. In addition, a surcharge of 14 percent is added to the in-house tariff.

The Singapore tourist office issues a brochure containing a list of budget hotels in the city centre. If the cost of the room is less than S$80, then it is a good idea to inspect the room before making a firm reservation. In Singapore, air-conditioning is indispensable.

Camping is possible on the island of Sentosa and hire-tents are available. The island also has two well-equipped youth hostels. For more information, contact Sentosa Information Office, World Trade Centre, tel: 275 0388.

The 'boutique' hotels, as they are known, are predominantly small- to medium-sized houses, often old colonial-style buildings in fairly peaceful locations.

The most popular hotels are undoubtedly the ones near Orchard Road (the main shopping street), in the city centre (Marina Square) or in Chinatown.

Hotel selection

The following are hotel suggestions for various quarters of the city. They are listed according to three categories: $$$ = expensive; $$ = moderate; $ = inexpensive.

Marina Mandarin: the atrium

93

View from the Westin Stamford

Singapore Marriot Hotel

Orchard Road district

$$$Four Seasons Hotel, 190 Orchard Boulevard, tel: 734 1110, fax: 733 0682. Design a strong feature. Good fitness suite. **$$$Goodwood Park Hotel**, 22 Scotts Road, tel: 737 7411, fax: 732 8558. One of the few hotels with charm and a sense of history. **$$$Grand Hyatt Hotel**, 10 Scotts Road, tel: 738 1234; fax: 732 1696. **$$–$$$Mandarin Singapore**, 333 Orchard Road, tel: 737 4411, fax: 738 2382. Over a thousand rooms; in the middle of Orchard Road. **$$–$$$The Regent Singapore**, 1 Cuscaden Road, tel: 733 8888, fax: 732 8838. Stylish with excellent service. **$$–$$$Singapore Marriot Hotel**, 320 Orchard Road, tel: 735 5800; fax: 735 9800. After extensive renovations, the only concession to the hotel's Chinese past is its pagoda roof. **$$ANAHotel**, 16 Nassim Hill, tel: 732 1222, fax: 732 2222. Run by the hospitality arm of All Nippon Airways, this is a quality business-class hotel situated atop a ridge.

City Centre (Marina Square)

$$$Raffles Hotel, 1 Beach Road, tel: 337 1886, fax: 339 7650. A residence rather than a hotel. The most expensive suites are furnished with carefully selected antiques (from S$700). **$$$Marina Mandarin**, 6 Raffles Boulevard, tel: 338 3388, fax: 845 1001. The 70-m (220-ft) high atrium is the biggest in southeast Asia. Try a cocktail here in the evening. Part of a busy shopping complex and linked by a corridor with the **$$$Pan Pacific Hotel Singapore**, 7 Raffles Boulevard, tel: 336 8111, fax: 339 1861. The glass lift gives a splendid view over the city centre and the Suntech City congress hall. **$$–$$$The Westin Stamford**, 2 Stamford Road, tel: 338 8585, fax: 338 2862. Within the luxurious Raffles City shopping centre. The tallest hotel in the world (226m/741ft) and the best view of Singapore's skyline. A room with a view must be booked well in